How to Organize and Maintain

the Library Picture/Pamphlet File

HOW TO
ORGANIZE AND MAINTAIN
THE LIBRARY
PICTURE / PAMPHLET FILE

by

GERALDINE N. GOULD

and

ITHMER C. WOLFE

Librarian, Walter Stillman School
Tenafly, New Jersey

1968 / **OCEANA PUBLICATIONS, INC.**

DOBBS FERRY, NEW YORK

Library of Congress Catalog Card Number 68-27154

PRINTED IN THE UNITED STATES OF AMERICA

Oceana Book No. 357

Foreword

In *How to Organize and Maintain the Library Picture/Pamphlet File,* the authors have approached one aspect of the problem of the development of school library service with a clear-cut understanding of the kinds of difficulties faced by staff members in the school and small public library. Even the professionally trained librarian, when available for appointment in such libraries which usually are even more limited in the amount of technical and clerical assistance than that allowed in larger libraries, may not have had the experience necessary to recognize and organize effectively the most essential services which such limitations may bring. Too, the literature of library science, voluminous though it may be, actually does not provide the school librarian in particular with specific blue-prints for action. Generally what does exist in written form consists of rather compressed statements of standards, some out-of-date handbooks and articles of topical interest.

Therefore, in examining this working manual for the management of a vertical file in the smaller library, it is a pleasure to discover that the information presented is so carefully selected and presented. The writers have defined the scope of the vertical file in the most meaningful sense of the term—"information" file—by expressly including in this school library resource not only clippings and pamphlets but also pictures, charts, maps and posters—in fact, almost any medium which can be collected, processed, circulated and housed in a "vertical" file. As such this handbook deals with materials that range through the many types of collections a library may have but which sometimes are so widely separated that their use by the school's clientele is impeded.

Finally, while the guidance for organizing and maintaining the vertical file presented here is addressed to the school, small public and religious library, it is quite likely that it will be used on a much wider scale as its precise, comprehensive and varied directions are more generally discovered.

Edward T. Schofield, Ed.D.
Director, Department of Libraries
and Audiovisual Education
Board of Education
Newark, New Jersey

Preface

I would have welcomed a publication such as this when I started the first vertical file of the elementary schools in Tenafly, New Jersey, thirteen years ago. So little had been published which fitted the needs of an elementary school library that I had to go to a number of libraries in New Jersey and in New York for guidance. Today, librarians are asking *us* for guidance.

At first reading, some of the procedures may seem overly complicated for the simple task of setting up a vertical file. We feel that a meticulously detailed description of how to set up and maintain a vertical file collection is essential if such a manual is to be truly useful. Actually, the details and the records which are suggested here lead to time saved in the end. We believe that with this guide, a vertical file can be established with much less effort than we have expended here in Tenafly.

Some librarians will adopt other methods. Certainly the needs and facilities of libraries are not all alike and some adaptation is always necessary. We have presented here, at length, what we in the Tenafly elementary schools regard as the best procedures for us. We have also described alternative methods which can be applied to other library situations whether they be elementary or secondary schools, small public, religious, or private libraries.

As Librarian, I have had to depend on PTA volunteers for the non-professional jobs in organizing and maintaining our vertical file. Their broad interests and contacts have proved extremely helpful. On the other hand, much time has been spent in supervising and in training many part-time people. I do not believe volunteers can take the place of a well-trained staff of paid clerks and secretaries. School systems should not be encouraged to make volunteers an excuse for failing to provide adequately trained staffs.

A few statistics may prove interesting. The Walter Stillman School in Tenafly, New Jersey, includes about 400 pupils, ranging from Kindergarten through Fifth Grades;

seventeen classroom teachers; one full-time librarian; and eight special teachers (who are shared with Tenafly's three other elementary schools).

At this writing, the vertical file consists of approximately 8,750 individual items (roughly 4,800 clippings and pamphlets; 3,100 mounted pictures; 670 oversized pieces; and 180 assorted professional items) filed under 712 subject headings.

In 1958, when the Stillman School file was still in the "carton stage" — and the school population was very much less than it is now—materials on seventy different subjects were circulated. Since then, our circulation has grown in keeping with the growth of the vertical file (and the school) with 317 subjects as the peak figure. These are numbers for *subjects only;* each subject incorporates a wealth of varied printed material (pictures, clippings, posters, maps, pamphlets, etc.). The total number of *pieces* circulated is considerably larger. In addition to the recorded circulation totals, twenty or more subjects may frequently be perused at the reading tables by a group of children. Naturally, their final selections taken out for further study will be substantially fewer and it is only this lesser number which is reflected in circulation totals.

It is not enough to "organize and maintain a vertical file." One also needs to encourage its use by making would-be users familiar with it. A good vertical file collection is an extremely valuable asset to any library, whether large or small. Publicizing its importance is but one of the many facets of the job of the librarian.

For the past nine years I have been Librarian at the Walter Stillman School. Time spent in establishing and in maintaining this vertical file collection has been most gratifying. It is my hope that this manual will constitute a guide to similarly rewarding experiences for other librarians in other libraries.

Ithmer C. Wolfe, Librarian
Walter Stillman School
Tenafly, New Jersey

Acknowledgments

On the professional level, the successful implementation of the vertical file concept in the Tenafly schools was greatly influenced by the invaluable efforts of Mrs. Eleanor Trimble, Librarian of J. Spencer Smith School.

Three librarians who were generous and helpful with their advice are Miss Romana Javits, Curator of the Picture Collection of the New York Public Library; Miss Marselle Frebault, Supervising Librarian (now retired), Art and Music Department, Newark Public Library; and Miss Bess Timmerman, Head of the Juvenile Department (now retired), Johnson Free Public Library, Hackensack, New Jersey. Without their guidance and encouragement, this project might never have been started.

We have had wonderful help from PTA volunteers in developing a vertical file collection which has been used with evident enthusiasm by children and by teachers. Particularly outstanding have been the contributions of Mrs. Vera Gillett and Mrs. Adina Gordon of J. Spencer Smith School and of Mrs. Carol Schults of Malcolm Mackay School.

Naturally, a step-by-step manual such as this cannot be prepared without the assistance and the support of others.

We owe many a thank-you to our husbands and to our children for their patience and their cooperation; to our library staff of volunteers who reassured us of the importance of the smallest details; to Mrs. Trimble for her superb "blue pencil."

Most of the photographs which appear in this manual are the work of Mr. Sol Feinstein, Audio-Visual Coordinator, Tenafly Public Schools.

The meticulous typing of the manuscript was done by Mrs. Mary Procita and Mrs. Margaret Fregans.

Finally, it is with most sincere appreciation that the authors of this manual acknowledge the encouragement and unstinting cooperation of Mr. Ernest J. Mueller, Principal of Walter Stillman School, as well as the gracious support of Dr. Carl B. Hoffman, Assistant Superintendent of Schools, Abington, Pennsylvania, and of Dr. John B. Geissinger, Superintendent of Schools, Tenafly, New Jersey.

G. N. G.

I. C. W.

Contents

I

Scope of the
Vertical File

Definition of Vertical File

In library parlance, the term "vertical file collection" pertains to printed, non-book reference materials which are housed vertically in file cabinets. The vertical file collection may contain any or all of the following: flat pictures, pamphlets, charts, maps, posters, newspaper and magazine clippings. Whether designated as a Vertical File Collection, Picture Collection, Pamphlet File, or Information File, it should be a permanent part of the library; collected and maintained by the librarian and her staff; utilized by borrowers seeking information.

Purposes of the Vertical File Collection

Vertical file collections help greatly to meet the varied demands on libraries since they provide kinds of material not always found in books. They permit selective coverage of some subjects which would have to be left out in a book collection of reasonable size. They may also provide adequate quantity and variety of materials on subjects of special interest.

Children's Use of the Vertical File

Good quality, carefully selected pictures help to present information in a most effective way, regardless of reading levels involved. For children, the vertical file has a magnetic attraction. Younger children, always responsive to perky illustrations, frequently are able to absorb information on their own level, in subjects normally considered beyond

their grasp. Librarians are accustomed to seeing the small child studying pictures for "fun." At times he senses the mood, at other times he enjoys the sheer beauty of the picture. He may be interested in how the artist draws or paints. He may look at a photograph to visualize an object. Being able to see a picture of an object, while discussing it, adds immeasurably to his learning and to his retention of that learning. As his knowledge and his experience increase, his observations and his ability to analyze increase.

Pamphlets can be superb—and often the only—sources of data not published in book form. In a typical instance, when a second grader and his family were about to move to a distant city, the best information they could locate was found in a booklet prepared by the Chamber of Commerce of that city and obtained by the librarian free of charge.

Older children make effective use of the vertical file in preparing their reports. It quite often provides a different approach to a subject from that which is found in available books, magazines, filmstrips, tapes, or films. The vertical file also helps to supply sufficient materials on certain subjects at peak periods. Although teachers are asked to check on available materials before giving assignments, and often do, there are times when any library is strained to fulfill the needs of all the students of one grade at one time.

For example, a teacher assigned a written report on the life of Robert E. Lee to eight children. Each report was to contain at least four references. The library had five complete books on his life, a number of books which contained some biographical data on him and three standard encyclopedias. An examination of the vertical file yielded three pamphlets on his life (one a duplicate), two leaflets highlighting places he had lived, and a manuscript copy of a letter he had written. These items, from the file, were enough to supply the material needed to complete the assignment.

Huge charts, maps, and posters cannot even be contained

FIGURE 3: When doing reports, children such as these fourth and fifth graders make use of pictures and pamphlets as well as books.

within the format of a book. One unforgettable experience occurred the afternoon the kindergartners of Stillman School were discussing John Glenn and his orbiting of the earth. They wanted to know what the universe was like.

Within twenty minutes, the children were studying pictures of the planets from books and from magazines, but their most exciting discovery was a chart from the oversized file which clearly showed the relative sizes of the planets and their distances from the sun. The children and their teacher could all look at it at once and talk about it together. That same afternoon the children made *papier maché* balls representing the planets and constructed their own solar system to hang from the ceiling.

Newspaper and magazine clippings are not only invaluable as sources of current world-wide information, but also as sources of local, specialized news and data. For instance, our vertical file contains several clippings from our local newspaper dealing with the water problems of Bergen

County (New Jersey) during the summer of 1965. There are photographs from the newspaper of local ponds and lakes which were severely affected by the drought conditions of that summer.

One lengthy newspaper article treats not only the drought, but also the pollution of a nearby river. Photographs within the article show the river in drought condition: its water level seriously lowered and its usually running waters still. Two more photographs show fish dying from lack of oxygen due to the presence of algae in the river. This particular river is quite familiar to most of our children. Hence, their study of water, as part of the conservation unit of fourth grade, is dramatically illustrated by the known and the commonplace.

Water pollution, water shortages, drought, and related problems are not academic theories in a text book, but very real, very close actualities.

FIGURE 4: High School level assignments are enriched by the use of timely Vertical File materials from many sources.

A library vertical file has the added virtue of helping to furnish a pattern for children to follow in establishing their own collections. Basic to learning is knowing how to organize materials in order to have them readily usable when needed. The technique needs to be taught in the elementary schools of today.

Teachers' Use of the Vertical File

A good teacher is always on the lookout for all sorts of materials with which to enhance his teaching. In time, he will collect some materials for his own use. The new teacher has not yet had the opportunity to do this. Therefore, the auxiliary teaching aids found in the vertical file are especially important to the new teacher. The experienced teacher often will find materials he has not seen or has no place to house himself. He is most grateful to the librarian for keeping him supplied as his needs arise. The vertical file becomes, for both new and experienced teachers, a quickly accessible repository for seldom used, but nonetheless vital, reference or secondary source material—immediately at hand when needed, conveniently stored out of the way when not.

Schools' Use of the Vertical File

The school halls, bulletin boards, and class display cases can be adorned with materials from the vertical file. It is an incomparable source of supply for graphic items which tie in with current events, special occasions, holidays, and specific units of study.

Libraries' Use of the Vertical File

The librarian may use the file constantly, within the library, to heighten interest in both new books and old favorites as well as to lead the way into new fields of interest.

FIGURE 5: The smallest detail on a vertical file item may prove to be of great value to the teacher as in this third grade lesson on COTTON.

FIGURE 6: The elementary school librarian can better help a teacher prepare for his next study unit when the library makes a full range of resources available: books, records, magazines, film strips, films, realia, and vertical file material.

Another most practical advantage of an effectively circulating vertical file collection is the manner in which outdated periodicals are employed. As every librarian knows, complete stacks of all magazines (even some of those with indexes) cannot be kept indefinitely within the library. However, numerous features remain timely and continue to evoke enough demand to warrant retention in some form. In such instances, articles may be cut from the magazines and incorporated into the vertical file collection.

FIGURE 7: United Nations Day is one of many occasions when the halls of the school need the facilities of the school library and its vertical file material.

Types of Material Collected

Naturally, the types of material and the subjects to be included in the vertical file collection depend upon the needs of each particular library. The vertical file usually does not duplicate information readily obtainable elsewhere in the library or, in the case of school libraries, within the classrooms. Its *raison d'etre* is to supply what is not immediately available or to graphically supplement what is. For instance, there are areas of interest which are not found in the book stacks of the library: either the books have not yet been purchased or the subject is too new and has not been published in suitable books. (What publisher, librarian, or annual budget can keep up with ARTIFICIAL SATELLITES?) Because the vertical file contains illustrative material, there are and will always be subjects which should be included despite satisfactory textual coverage elsewhere. Furthermore, in cases where unusual quantities of material on a specific subject are likely to be needed at one time, some duplication of text is always advisable.

With specific reference to school libraries, the sorts of materials which are most apt to be used are dictated by individual school curriculums and by teachers' needs. Many schools have curriculum outlines which should be consulted to provide guidelines in the general selection of subject matter for the vertical file.

Since there is a strong emphasis on social studies in the schools, this may be a good place to start the basic collection. Using the social studies outline as a general guide, the librarian will see the almost unlimited scope of subject matter which must be included in the vertical file collection. *Just as classroom discussion can meander seemingly far afield but yet remain within the teacher's lesson plan, so, too, must the subject matter within the vertical file be broad and varied.*

Equal in importance to the social studies program for the vertical file are the science subjects. Librarians will discover that each science unit serves as a core around which to build a superbly diversified collection. These two major units, social studies and science, nucleus of the vertical file, lead to other prime interest subjects.

Further examples of subjects and of materials which add

FIGURE 8: The hall display case adjacent to the library uses vertical file pictures to highlight books of interest to all grades.

FIGURE 9: During a story hour for the first grade, the librarian employs mounted pictures (as well as realia) to help define and illustrate new concepts to the youngsters.

FIGURE 10: Sixth grade reading assignments are enhanced by vertical file materials. (It is important to be able to identify what belongs to whom when the display is dismantled since the teacher's own items may be similar to those of the library.)

to the value of the school vertical file collection are reproductions of fine art for the art classes, measurement charts
for the arithmetic classes, nutrition posters for health study,
and so forth. The list is virtually endless. Anything which
can conceivably add to the presentation of any particular
subject is potential vertical file material.

Just as the book collection of any library is as broad as
imagination, funds, and space permit, so must be its vertical
file. For those children with highly specialized interests and
for those children deeply involved with various extra-cur-
ricular activities, the library should provide material in the
vertical file which does not necessarily bear directly on
school subjects. There is always a demand for the latest
information on skin-diving, annual softball regulations, training of pets, building of model ships . . . and the feeding of
skinks. Obviously, the vertical file can—and should—be as
full of pure enjoyment as it is of hardcore information.

FIGURE 11: A fourth grade exhibit colorfully combines various
types of library vertical file material with children's own
reports and projects.

Weeding the Vertical File Collection

While planning vertical file collections, librarians should bear in mind the fact that flexibility is basic to their structure. Just as the catalog of any library can easily become choked with no longer useful or desirable titles, so can the vertical file become encumbered with no longer pertinent items or subjects. It is relatively simple to keep a vertical file collection up-to-date and relevant. New materials can be added with little effort; those which are no longer useful can be even more easily discarded in the "circular file." Since vertical file materials are not cataloged by individual items but only by subject, catalog cards are withdrawn only when *all* material is retired from a specific subject unit.

Scope of Manual

Librarians are often unaware of the wealth of good pictures, pamphlets, charts, etc., which can be secured through magazine features, advertisements and advertising literature, domestic and foreign commissions, and the good-will promotional publications of American industries. These sources can, and do, supply magnificently prepared visual aids which help to create an effective library resource. The widespread availability of such superb materials, at little cost, means that library budgets can go farther than might otherwise be possible with the funds which have been allocated for such materials. This manual therefore emphasizes the procedures which can be followed in selecting, obtaining, and evaluating such materials.

Catharine M. Williams, in her book, *Learning from Pictures,*[1] lists thirty-one "instructional purposes served by pictures." It is not the purpose of this manual to elaborate

---

[1] Catharine M. Williams, *Learning from Pictures,* Washington, D.C., National Education Association, 1963, pp. 5-17.

FIGURES 12 - 16: Two closely inter-related study units, FORESTS AND FORESTRY and LUMBER AND LUMBERING, illustrate the many and varied types of free material available for school use for just the cost of a postage stamp: vertical file pictures culled from myriad sources . . .

FIGURE 13: . . . beautifully printed, informative pamphlets from many different sources . . .

FIGURE 14: . . . attractive oversized posters and charts supplied to the schools by private industry and the United States Government . . .

FIGURE 15: . . . pamphlets, study guides, statistical bulletins, playlets, all supplied free of charge, for professional use . . .

FIGURE 16: . . . even actual photographs, supplied by industry, which demonstrate the use of machinery in forestry operations.

on the educational merits of flat pictures. In the past few years, excellent materials have been published which will guide the librarian or teacher in the techniques of instruction with pictures. The aim of this manual is to give guidance to the librarian in the processing and the organizing of pictures (and other vertical file material) so that they are readily available for use by the borrowers.

Finally, maximum use will be made of the file collection if it is competently designed and systematized from its inception. To assist the librarian in her initial planning, this manual deals at length with the housing of vertical file materals, as well as cataloging and circulation procedures.

Since contemporary libraries are true "materials centers," librarians must supervise the handling of numerous different types of items. Although the procedures described on the following pages deal exclusively with printed matter, many of the recommendations may be applied to other visual teaching aids. Form and housing may differ, but the problems of subject headings, cataloging, and circulation are essentially the same. Therefore, with some adaptation to suit local requirements, the librarian concerned with other non-book materials will find much of interest and of help.

II

Establishing the Vertical File Collection

Developing and maintaining a good vertical file collection is largely dependent upon availability of time. Few librarians, with their manifold duties, have the hours needed to expand into this increasingly important field without help. Accordingly, with proper instructions and supervision, clerks must do much of the routine work. In any event, paying librarian's wages for cutting and pasting is poor economy. In school libraries, "volunteer mothers" can be of real service; and student assistants can be given specific, simple duties.

Professional and Non-Professional Duties

From the beginning, it is important for the librarian to plan procedures and allocate specific jobs. The table (page 22) indicates a typical work schedule which can be adapted to individual situations.

Using volunteers in various capacities within the school library is certainly not a novel nor an unusual approach. With specific reference to the vertical file, however, experience with volunteers has shown that they add a dimension to the collection that the librarian, regardless of the extent of her contacts and experience, cannot.

Vertical File Committee

However, experience also has shown that there are severe drawbacks to working with volunteers in the school library. Since volunteers are, at most, available only for a comparatively few short years (between the entrance of their children into and graduation from the school), the librarian will find that she will probably have to train new volunteers

WORK FUNCTIONS°

Professional	Non-Professional (Clerks or Volunteers)	Student Assistants °°
Evaluate and purchase selection tools		
Select sources to be explored	Type letters to sources; inventory received items	
	Preliminarily select items for inclusion in collection	
Appraise material received; — to be mounted		
	Process all material	Stamp ownership on all material
Assign subject headings	Enter subject headings on all material; type catalog cards °°°	
		File all material
Check filing for accuracy		
	Weeding of collection	
Evaluate weeded material		

° Circulation is handled in the normal manner, consistent with general library routine.
°° Depending upon age levels, students may assume one or more of the duties in Column II.
°°° Catalog cards are filed as directed by librarian or in accordance with library practice.

each school year. Such lack of continuity from year to year is a serious waste of the librarian's precious time. In addition, few volunteers will have anything but the most rudimentary knowledge of library procedures. Although members of the vertical file volunteer committee function within a limited and relatively restricted area of responsibility, a working knowledge of the broader scope of the basic routine of libraries is necessary for an over-all appreciation of what is to be accomplished.

The most discouraging aspect of all, in working with volunteers, is the inescapable fact that many will start the work, discover that they do not care for it, and resign, leaving the committee severely under-staffed and unable to continue their operations smoothly. Many well meaning volunteers begin, but do not take their commitments seriously. On the other hand, there are those who are sincere, but have little or no ability. These are just as difficult to work with as those who are erratic in their schedules.

However, let it be noted that there are no substitutes for the able, dedicated volunteer. She will grasp fundamental principles quickly; she will be dependable; she will work extra-long hours during peak pressure periods; she will work without regard to holidays and hours-off; no aspect of the job will be beneath her. This volunteer is relatively rare, but well worth whatever time is spent in training her.

Should the librarian decide to work with a committee of volunteers, the following suggests specific ways in which the committee could function. In other library situations, such non-professional jobs would be handled by library clerks.

An ideal committee consists of a chairman and about six members. It is essential that the chairman become familiar with the general course of study and know what subject material is likely to be needed.

At first, of course, it will be necessary for the librarian

to work closely with the chairman. In time, however, an avid volunteer will be able to grasp enough of basic vertical file principles to continue on a daily basis without constant supervision. At least one of the members of the working committee should be a fairly good typist in order to handle the correspondence, labeling, and card catalog entries.

Volunteers should be cautioned not to attempt to guess at what would attract a child since this takes more formal training than most non-professional women have. (The busy librarian usually does not have time to provide such training to the group.) However, since these are mothers of school-age children, they are not too far removed from the broad spectrum of interest to their youngsters and, generally, can be relied upon for their intuitive reactions.

Some volunteers may have highly developed interests in specific fields which, surprisingly enough, can actually work to the benefit of the vertical file. Keen awareness of a particular topic, with adequate guidance from the librarian, can lead to the inclusion into the vertical file of a diversity of subjects which might otherwise be lacking.

FIGURE 17: Mounting• pictures at home can be the perfect answer for those who wish to volunteer for library work but who may not be available during school hours.

Since much of the material probably will not be formally requested through written correspondence, but will be found in miscellaneous magazines, books, newspapers, etc., it will be necessary to train the non-professional worker to look for and to recognize *potentially* useful material. There will be discouragingly huge masses of such items to be scanned for preliminary selection. Obviously, the librarian can not, and should not, expend her energies in this direction; she should save herself for the final decision of what is or is not to be included in the vertical file collection.

With the following questions in mind, discussion ends and day-to-day execution techniques begin .

Selection Criteria

In selecting both pictorial and textual material for inclusion in the vertical file collection, four points are emphasized:

1. INTEREST: Is it appealing? If textual, is it well-written, its presentation readily understandable? Is the type clear, the text readable? If pictorial, are important details easily discernable? If in color, is the color true?

2. INTEGRITY: Is it truthful? If subject is controversial, are all sides fairly and objectively presented? If political, is the message presented without bias and without propaganda? If it contains advertising, is the self-promotional aspect limited and subdued, not blatant? If statistical, is the data accurate? Is its viewpoint contemporary, not quaintly "dated"? If pictorial, is it natural, not coyly picturesque or obviously "posed"? Are details valid, accurate for subject depicted? Contemporary? Historical?

3. IMAGINATION: Does it stimulate thought? Induce further research? Is it informative? Factual? Is it fanciful? Whimsical? Will it encourage further reading?

4. IMMEDIACY: Does it fill a specific current need, or

does it duplicate other materials in the library? Does it fulfill its function well, or can a better one be found? On "second look," does it retain its pertinence and vitality?

Despite all tests which might be devised for a picture, a pamphlet, a clipping, or other vertical file items, there will be missed opportunities and erroneous judgments. Items will be rejected which should have been included in the collection; items will be included for which there will be no use. Fortunately, because of the basic structure of vertical file collections, most such errors can be corrected. A careful search may very well lead back to that discarded booklet or chart; diligent reading of the file will uncover unwanted, space-taking materials.

III
Collecting
Material

The first pictures will be obtained from innumerable free outlets available to school libraries. The file can be built from such sources for the first year, depending upon the speed with which the staff works. It takes at least this long to garner a basic collection, to process pieces, and to see them in action. Only at this point, when free sources have been fully exploited and when the librarian has become more familiar with the general type of literature made accessible to schools, will she be in a position to judge the true merit of items for which charges are made.

Magazines

Without doubt, the bulk of the initial subjects will come from magazines because they are the medium most commonly received. When the project becomes known to the local population, all sorts of magazines will be brought in. In some instances, the public library is often able and willing to contribute suitable periodicals to such a project in the schools. At the start, most will yield something of value. As the file grows in content and in breadth, however, general magazines will grow progressively less rewarding (although picture periodicals will always be a mainstay).

In addition, both general and special interest magazines frequently offer free or inexpensive material to their readership. Much of this literature can prove helpful for school and public library use.

Within the magazines, advertisements and feature articles are equally productive. The collector, in going through the pages of popular magazines, needs an almost immediate "eye" for the potential of a picture and must be able to visualize how "cropping out" extraneous elements can desirably alter illustrations.

When working with current publications, one should have two copies available for cutting, if at all possible. Since many desirable pictures and articles often are printed on both sides of a page, one of the sides will be concealed when the sheet is mounted. In order to effectively cull all information from the issue, it is then necessary to use alternate pages from each copy to avoid sacrificing essential details.

Miscellaneous Printed Matter

Calendars, direct mail advertising pieces, well-printed picture post cards, discarded encyclopedias, etc., are all likely candidates for vertical file material. In fact, when once under way, the collector uncovers subject material in the most unexpected places.

In the search for well produced pictures from readily obtainable materials, the librarian may wish to consider purchasing both hard- and soft-bound "picture" books which can be cut up for this purpose. Obviously, no general rule can be applied to using this approach, for the needs of each library differ widely. The librarian will have to consider the merits of this proposal based on the particular requirements of individual subject areas. For instance, this is often a less expensive way to collect fine art reproductions than by buying individual pictures. Similarly, well-produced travel, geographic, and natural history magazines generally are cheaper sources of picture needs for numerous study units.

Newspapers

Newspapers are especially valuable as sources of local information: historical background, contemporary events, unusual weather conditions and related natural phenomena, native celebrities, etc. Items taken from newspapers should be selected carefully and with discretion because the reproduction is low grade, the paper too fragile and short lived for long term use. However, if the item is extremely important for a specific unit, it can be incorporated if it is mounted promptly.

Students' Own Work

In school libraries, it is suggested that the file does not include original work by students: reports, drawings, projects, book reports, et. al. There is usually ample space for display of their works both inside the library and in the school halls and cases. Accordingly, rather than disappoint a single would-be contributor, it may be helpful to establish a blanket rule that no student art work contributions are accepted. On the other hand, students can be a productive, eager source for new material and should be encouraged to donate from all standard printed media to which they have access. For example, students, while preparing their reports, occasionally unearth previously untapped sources of information. In addition, while on extended travels with their parents, children frequently will come upon unpublicized materials which can greatly enhance the vertical file collection.

Commercial Picture Sets

School librarians, particularly, may wish to investigate the number of picture sets (for use in the opaque projector) which have long been available commercially. In black-and-white or in color, such sets are geared to the science, social studies, and art study units of schools. Some individual pictures are large enough to be used in classroom discussion without the opaque projector. In addition, commercial pictures are excellent bulletin board material.

Guides to Free Material

The library should invest in one or two of the many guides to free material which are geared to the curriculum needs of schools (see *APPENDIX D*). Such guides, arranged alphabetically by subject, contain an extensive list of materials which are available free to schools and to libraries from sources located in the United States. Since the availability of such free material is subject to frequent change, it is strongly urged that librarians work only with current editions of source guides. A new and different guide, purchased every second year (or a revised edition of a previously acquired guide purchased every third year) is normally sufficient for the needs of the small library.

Trade Associations

Trade associations (dairy, lumber, etc.), most of which can be found listed in the guides, are veritable gold mines of teaching aids. When specific information is required in specific fields, primary contacts should be made with the representative industrial, trade, or professional groups.

Private Industry

Aside from their listings in free and inexpensive source guides, many business firms offer reprints of their advertisements and other related printed matter. When an attractive and potentially useful advertisement is found, a letter written to the advertiser may prove rewarding.

United States Government Agencies

Government bureaus (U. S. Department of the Interior, U. S. Coast Guard, U. S. Atomic Energy Commission, etc.) offer a host of materials in numerous areas of study. However, the majority of United States government publications are textual and do not enrich the file, pictorially. These can be extremely valuable in the junior or senior high school and public libraries, but one must search to find the few materials written on elementary grade levels. At the same time, certain subject areas such as Indians, parks, fish, wildlife and forestry have materials which can be used in the elementary school.

Nevertheless, the latest statistics and facts commonly found in these bulletins are highly prized by the teaching staff, although the information itself later is presented on

FIGURE 18: For advanced level research, United States Government pamphlets provide immediacy as well as authoritative data.

grade levels. Therefore, the value of the vertical file collection might be increased if it contains a section solely for faculty, or professional use. Such a division, consisting of miscellaneous items (teachers' reading and study guides, scripts for class plays, holiday songs, etc.), would naturally require the inclusion of many United States government publications.

Local government (state, county, community) publications, on the other hand, should be included almost without reservation. Although such bulletins may need extensive interpretation by the librarian or by the teacher for the younger pupil, the data and historical details in these documents—usually unavailable elsewhere—should not be bypassed.

Frequently, material will be received which contains bibliographies which can be used as guides to additional visual teaching aids. By all means, they should be explored.

IV

Soliciting and
Sorting Material

Source guides for free and inexpensive materials probably will be the foundations of vertical file correspondence.

Mimeographed Letters of Request

To ease the burden which mass letter writing can be, a well composed and neatly mimeographed form letter is useful. *All* letters *must* be on official library or school letterheads. While the main body of the letter is mimeographed, the date and inside address are hand typed and the librarian's signature is *always* hand written. Contrary to all expert advice opposed to mechanical processing for letters of this nature, experience definitely has proven that high-quality mimeographing coupled with these various personalizing details, will produce excellent results.

A typical letter is reproduced in *Figure 19*. Make special note of the fact that the appeal incorporates a detailed explanation of the manner in which the requested items will be used and of the desire for free items. In a personally typed postscript, always ask for two copies if pamphlets are being requested. This is necessary should the librarian decide that (1) the pamphlet will be more useful if its pages are cut and mounted individually, (2) one copy is to be cut and one copy saved intact, or (3) the demand for it may be heavy enough to warrant duplicate copies.

Naturally, any form letter will have to be adapted to the individual situation of each school library.

For school libraries, it is a most economical method, requiring little further effort, for one librarian to collect the core of the vertical file for the entire school system. Each school library processes and maintains its own file and, when

TENAFLY   PUBLIC   SCHOOLS

TENAFLY, N. J 07670

March 2, 1968

Diamond Crystal Salt Company
St. Clair, Michigan

Gentlemen:

We are currently engaged in enlarging our "teaching aids" file of illustrated material that is meant to be of interest and assistance to our pupils in grades Kindergarten through Sixth and their teachers.

Any illustrated wall charts, pamphlets, or reprints which you are in a position to donate to this program will certainly be most gratefully appreciated.

These will be part of our permanent library files, circulated exclusively by our library staff members exactly in the way our bound reference volumes are.

It would help if you would <u>address</u> <u>the</u> <u>material</u> <u>to</u> <u>my</u> <u>attention</u>, as indicated below, so that we can avoid misdirection at this end.

Thank you for any assistance you can provide.

Very truly yours,

Ithmer M. Wolfe

(Mrs.) Ithmer M. Wolfe, Librarian
WALTER STILLMAN SCHOOL
Tenafly Road
Tenafly, New Jersey 07670

FIGURE 19

once established, can then follow through on individual requests as needs arise. The written requests will have to state
clearly that material is sought for each of the schools. Unless
stock is severely limited, sources are usually most cooperative. A mimeographed form (*Figure 20*), stapled to the letter
which is being sent will suffice.

In the interests of economy and to save you undue
handling expenses, may we request <u>four</u> of <u>each</u> item
you choose to send to us? In this way, all four of
our elementary schools will receive your material
and you will be spared the labor of replying to four
individual inquiries. Again . . . thank you.

FIGURE 20

Individually Typed Letters of Request

Of course, while a form is suitable for the bulk of the
correspondence, there will be instances when personally
typed letters are more appropriate and productive. (For
example, when the librarian has a unique or special request,
seeks specific subjects, or requires some sort of guidance
from the organization addressed, the standard form will have
to be adapted.)

It has been found that individually typed letters bring a
better response from foreign embassies and from (United
States) state associations (see *APPENDIX A*).

When letters such as these are received by the addressee,
they will be handled in a routine way unless the letter
clearly requires more intensive treatment.

The letter should state *precisely* what is wanted, otherwise the response may well be unsatisfactory: tourist material or industrial development literature may be received
which, while sufficiently informative for general needs, may
not be suitable for the subjects the librarian is actually in-
tending to collect.

The sample letters, reproduced here (*Figures 21 and 22*),

TENAFLY PUBLIC SCHOOLS

TENAFLY, N. J. 07670

February 12, 1968

Netherlands Information Service
711 Third Avenue
New York 17, New York

Gentlemen:

In order to meet our expanding Social Studies' needs, we are
enlarging our "teaching aids" file of illustrated materials
pertaining to The Netherlands. These items are meant to be
of interest and assistance to our pupils in grades Kindergarten
through Sixth and their teachers.

Much of the material we presently have regarding The Netherlands
has been culled from periodicals such as "National Geographic" and
"Life" magazines. We are now attempting to complete our reference
files with pictures and posters which accurately portray the every-
day life of the people of The Netherlands ...urban as well as
rural; its industries as well as its handicrafts; its historical
landmarks as well as its scenic beauties.

For our primary grades, material which deals with your children and
their pets, homes, schools (both contemporary and historical), and
their recreation will be most welcome.

Any illustrated wall charts, pamphlets, or reprints which you are
in a position to donate to this program will certainly be most
gratefully appreciated.

These will be part of our permanent library files, circulated
exclusively by our library staff members exactly in the way our
bound reference volumes are.

It would help if you would address the material to my attention,
as indicated below, so that we can avoid misdirection at this end.

Very truly yours,

Ithmer M. Wolfe

(Mrs.) Ithmer M. Wolfe, Librarian
WALTER STILLMAN SCHOOL
Tenafly Road
Tenafly, New Jersey 07670

FIGURE 21

TENAFLY PUBLIC SCHOOLS

TENAFLY, N. J. 07670

February 23, 1968

South Carolina State Development Board
Advertising and Public Relations Dept.
P. O. Box 927
Columbia, South Carolina 29202

Gentlemen:

In order to meet our expanding Social Studies'
needs, we are enlarging our "teaching aids" file of illustrated
materials pertaining to South Carolina. These items are meant
to be of interest and assistance to our pupils in grades
Kindergarten through Sixth and to their teachers.

At this time, we are primarily interested in
informative and visually appealing material which illustrates
not only the scenic attractions and historical background of
South Carolina, but also its natural resources and economic
development.

Any posters, wall charts, or pamphlets which you
are in a position to donate to this program will certainly be
most appreciated.

If your office cannot furnish us with such material,
is it possible for you to forward our request to an agency that
can do so?

It would help, too, if you would address the material
to my attention, as indicated below, so that we can avoid misdirection at this end.

Thank you for any assistance which you can provide.

Very truly yours,

Ithmer M. Wolfe

(Mrs.) Ithmer M. Wolfe, Librarian
WALTER STILLMAN SCHOOL
Tenafly Road
Tenafly, New Jersey 07670

FIGURE 22

are explicit about what is wanted for an elementary school library. The appearance and the tone of the letters warrant careful consideration by the recipients and the letters usually receive it.

The use of standard window envelopes will eliminate a second addressing operation, thereby substantially saving time and labor.

Post Cards

Post cards work reasonably well although the response rate is usually about 20% lower than that attained by the standard form letter. Post cards can be used when mailing requests for free material to sources listed in the material guides.

There may be well over one hundred separate addresses written to at one time and the labor involved in individual letters, added to the cost of first class mail, would make it a prohibitive chore. Although the response rate may be somewhat lowered by the use of cards, enough additions will be gained for the files to make this procedure worthwhile. If

---

January 26, 1968

Sirs:

We would greatly appreciate receiving, for our permanent files, the following free material as listed in THE ELEMENTARY TEACHERS GUIDE:

HEALTH THROUGH THE AGES (two copies, if possible)

Thank you so much for your kind cooperation.

Stillman School Library

(Mrs.) Ithmer M. Wolfe,
Librarian
WALTER STILLMAN SCHOOL
Tenafly, New Jersey 07670

Please address to my attention!

FIGURE 23

the librarian is writing for additional material for other schools, as mentioned above, this fact should be noted on the post card. (United States government agencies always reply to post cards.) *Figure 23* is an example of a typical post card sent to sources which are listed in the guides to free material. Again, note the personal signature and the official library stamp.

Signature Key

Mass-mailings—whether mimeographed or hand-typed, on letterheads or on post cards, for one library or several—result in a flood of responses. Unless the staff is well-prepared in advance, vertical file mail becomes virtually indistinguishable from the normal, daily correspondence and catalogues which are addressed to the librarian or to the library. Sorting the two types then becomes a major, time-consuming chore in itself. Since it is not always possible to go through all of the incoming mail immediately, important letters and bibliographical lists sometimes are "lost." On the other hand, the librarian frequently finds that she is opening mail which is not her concern—yet.

In order to avoid such confusion, vertical file mail must have some sort of unique identifying mark when it is sent from the source to the library. Mail in plain envelopes, with nothing but a street or a box number, is impossible to identify. Further, since many sources also address the librarian on matters which do not pertain to the vertical file, even the company name on the outside of the envelope may not be sufficient identification. The solution to the problem, however, is quite simple: use a "key." The key, when properly handled, will be all that is needed to immediately recognize vertical file responses—without having to waste precious time in opening envelopes.

This magic key is nothing more than an initial added to the signature of the librarian on all correspondence addressed to potential vertical file sources. For example: if the librarian is "Jane Doe," her signature can then become "Jane V. Doe." The "V." is the key—the signal—which alerts her staff to the fact that "this particular piece of mail is for the vertical file and is not to be confused with her regular mail." Naturally, if "Jane Doe" already uses a middle initial in her formal signature, she will have to select a different one for her key ("Jane L. Doe" can then become "Jane V. Doe"). A glance at the cover of this manual will show that one of the authors, Librarian of Stillman School, is Ithmer C. Wolfe. A further glance (at *Figures 19-23*) will uncover the fact that Ithmer *M*. Wolfe sends requests for vertical file material.

There is one other factor to note in these sample letters and post card. *All* of them emphatically state "Please address reply to my attention!" The purpose of this is two-fold: (1) to make certain that all mail for the vertical file is addressed to the librarian, by name, thereby ensuring the use of the signature key on the envelope, and (2) to avoid the misdirection of incoming mail if first it is delivered to a central office before its final distribution.

Inventory and Reference File

An inventory/reference file, kept in conjunction with correspondence, is an essential supplementary tool which functions in numerous ways.

CORRESPONDENCE CONTROL

As a correspondence control file, it is a running record of requests that are outstanding. Through the years, literally hundreds of vertical file letters and cards will be mailed and many more hundreds of individual pieces received in answer. In the beginning, memory may serve, but as the file grows more complex there will be confusion and doubt as to what has been received, from whom and when.

QUALITY EVALUATION

Further than this, however, all individual sources are evaluated as to quality and aptness of material which they have sent. A handy, permanent index is imperative so that requests are not repeatedly sent to inappropriate or unproductive sources. If a source does not answer, or fails to send material for any number of reasons, this too is noted, thereby avoiding future, wasted efforts.

REFERENCE FILE

As a reference file, it is the library's individual resource guide for patrons who require current reference materials. Should a borrower desire a particular type of visual aid on a specific subject, the possibility of its availability can be speedily checked. If the librarian would like to obtain additional copies of any specific item in the vertical file, all qualifying information pertaining to the likelihood of its availability is at hand. Frequently, borrowers call the librarian's attention to, and suggest that she send for, items about which they have just heard or read. An up-to-date inventory/reference file is easily checked, in such instances, to see if the specific source has already been utilized for this specific material. In this aspect, it is a thoroughly efficient labor and cost saving tool.

RECORD OF CORRESPONDENCE

On its simplest level, it is a complete catalog of all vertical file correspondence from the very start of the project. The personnel of the vertical file may change over a period of time. In due course, some of the original staff may be unreachable for answering questions pertaining to correspondence and to sources. Therefore, the need for a written record of what action has been taken becomes a readily apparent necessity. It is easier to keep the records from the beginning than to have to start later on, thereby duplicating previous efforts.

In short, this is a file with many differing applications as well as a broad spectrum of supplementary uses. Despite its undramatic appearance, it is indispensable. In actuality, the backs of old and retired catalog cards can be used. The common carton in which they are shipped, so like a small file drawer, can be used for storing. Not only does this represent an economy for the library, but it is also a convenient utilization of materials. The physical appearance of the inventory/reference file is unimportant. It is a necessity upon which undue valuable energy and time need not be expended. It is rarely used by visitors to the library. However, the information entered on each card of this particular file must be intelligible to all involved with its use.

The file box is divided into three sections:
Pending Correspondence
Source Records
Subject Records

PENDING CORRESPONDENCE

When a request for material is sent, a card is immediately filled in and filed alphabetically, by name of addressee, in this section. A note should be made if a specific request was sent. A notation of the date the letter was written is helpful. At this point, the card will be similar to the one illustrated in *Figure 24*.

SOURCE RECORDS

When a reply is received, add the following information to the original, or basic, card:

1. Nature of reply.
2. Nature and quality of packet received.
3. Subject heading under which material is to be filed in vertical file cabinet.

```
Allis-Chalmers Mfg. Co.
Farm Equipment Div.
Adv. Dept.
Milwaukee 1, Wisc.


2/68
```

FIGURE 24

The basic card then looks something like the one shown below before it is refiled under the new category:

```
                                    AGRICULTURAL MACHINERY

        Allis-Chalmers Mfg. Co.
        Farm Equipment Div.
        Adv. Dept.
        Milwaukee 1, Wisc.

        2/68
```
" Man & Food CHARTS". OVERSIZED; VF; TEACHER'S GUIDE, EXCELLENT INFO.; COLOR ILLUS.

FIGURE 25

Subject Records

Upon receipt of material for which the correspondent has sent, one or more cards may be needed (depending upon the number of subjects covered by each item in the package). They are simple cards: in the upper right hand corner is the vertical file subject heading; the source(s) name(s) listed below it in a column to the left. Consequently, when it then becomes necessary, at some future date, to locate suppliers of items pertaining to a specific unit, all source names are conveniently listed under the category. As an auxiliary cross-reference, the source records division contains all necessary data (such as: address, type of material available, quality of items, etc.) needed in the exploitation of any one supplier.

This is a hard working section despite its unimpressive appearance since any special source can be located in a moment—whether it be a pamphlet on the care of turtles or a geodetic map of Maine.

Figures 26 and 27 illustrate average subject records cards. Note two points:

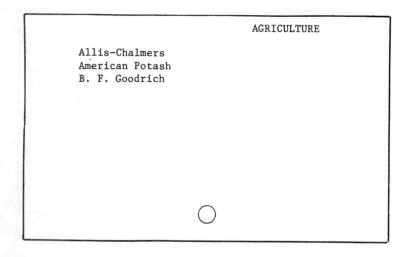

FIGURE 26

1. The subject heading is identical with that in the vertical file and card catalog.

2. The items sent by two of the corporations are useful in more than one category.

```
                              AGRICULTURAL MACHINERY

      Allis-Chalmers
      B. F. Goodrich
      International Harvester
```

FIGURE 27

"Dead Sources"

Inevitably, no matter how productive vertical file correspondence may be, there will be "no-answers." There is no accurate way to determine the precise reasons for a "no answer" or "dead request." As noted earlier, post cards are undoubtedly partially responsible. In addition, organizations and industries cannot always reply if "out-of-stock" or if the literature has been permanently discontinued. This is understandable since the expense of individual responses to the public would be far too costly—even for our cooperative American industry.

Nonetheless, because material is often in the process of being reprinted for free distribution and will again be available, allow a full year before considering a lead "dead." At this time, move the basic card from the "pending" section into the source records section. In time, it will save many hours which might otherwise be wasted on unfruitful letter-sending. Occasionally, a notation indicating what was written to the addressee and why no answer was received (if known) may prove helpful for future reference. Below is a "dead" file card which indicates what was requested (*Figure 28*).

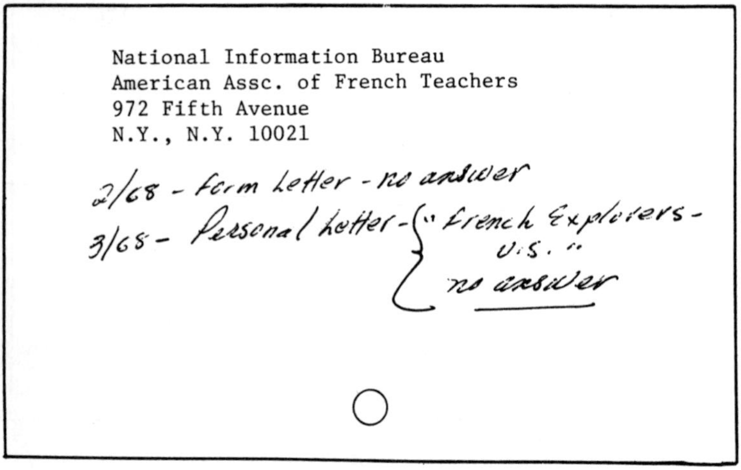

National Information Bureau
American Assc. of French Teachers
972 Fifth Avenue
N.Y., N.Y. 10021

2/68 - form Letter - no answer
3/68 - Personal Letter - ("French Explorers - U.S." no answer

FIGURE 28

Alternate Procedures

Although at first reading the above may seem somewhat complicated and time consuming, it is, on the contrary, a time-saver. It has come to be considered an integral part of the record-keeping of the library since the various alternatives have serious deficiencies:

1. Qualifying notes may be written directly in the margins of each guide, opposite sources which have been solicited.

   The drawback to this is threefold: comments can be too lengthy, at times, for marginal notations; if the librarian is using a number of guides, finding the original reference becomes an almost impossible chore; some method would have to be devised to include sources which are not listed in any guide.

2. The material itself can be examined, in the files, in order to check against duplication or to determine suitability.

The defect in this approach is that if the material has been retired or is in circulation, there is no way of judging its aptness. In addition, this second method does not help to ascertain whether or not the item had been received and was discarded because it lacked pertinence.

3. Material can be ordered without regard to previous action.

While this does away with *all* record-keeping, it represents an undue waste of labor, supplies, and funds.

In actual practice, an inventory/reference file takes but little extra effort. Kept in conjunction with vertical file correspondence, it is an almost indispensable record of previous action and is equally useful as a guide for future action.

There is no real necessity for keeping a running record of other than correspondence sources. Periodicals can always be checked in *The Readers' Guide to Periodical Literature*. Items which have been paid for are noted elsewhere in normal purchasing records. All else, such as post cards, isolated calendar pictures, etc., come upon by chance, are too elusive to merit any sort of attempt at permanent recording.

Incoming Mail

If the primary mailing was to a sizeable number of sources, the quantity of incoming mail may very well turn an orderly library workroom into utter chaos.

At this point, the first thing to do is to separate the numerous pieces of mail while designating what is to be done with them.

Duplicate Materials

If the school librarian is collecting duplicates for other schools in the system, they should be marked as such and put aside—out of the way—as quickly as possible.

"Above-Grade" Materials

For the school library, there will be much that is not usable despite all precautions and attempts at selective screening. Elementary school librarians should make it standard practice to pass "above-grade' units on to the junior and senior high schools, or the public library. The public librarian, on the other hand, should pass her unusable "grade" units on to the appropriate school. At that time, they should be treated as are the duplicates and should be placed aside promptly. A corner of the workroom, with boxes appropriately marked, will suffice until sufficient quantities have been accumulated to forward periodically.

Realia

If realia (three-dimensional objects) have been received, they should be promptly turned over to the one responsible for their cataloging.

Decorative Posters

Travel posters sometimes do not directly contribute to the teaching of the areas represented. Nevertheless, they are too attractive and imaginative to simply discard. These can be passed on to community organizations or to school "prop" departments for use in class plays, PTA affairs, et. al.

Usable Materials

All that now remains is vertical file material: pamphlets, pictures, posters, etc. A second and more critical perusal at this time will determine which items are to be kept for the vertical file; which are ready for subject headings just as they are; which will need further attention from the staff.

Pamphlets

Pamphlets are easily processed and quickly put into circulation (see pages 71-75). Without doubt, there will be a number of pamphlets which ostensibly do not seem to fill the requirements of the library. However, on closer scrutiny, it may develop that the *pictures* are worth saving. These should be noted and, at this time, put with the material to be mounted.

Picture Material

Picture material is culled from the mail and evaluated now also. Those which are not to be mounted, for one reason or another, are treated like pamphlets and clippings.

Oversized Items

Oversized items which are to be retained and filed (see Chapter IX) are marked accordingly.

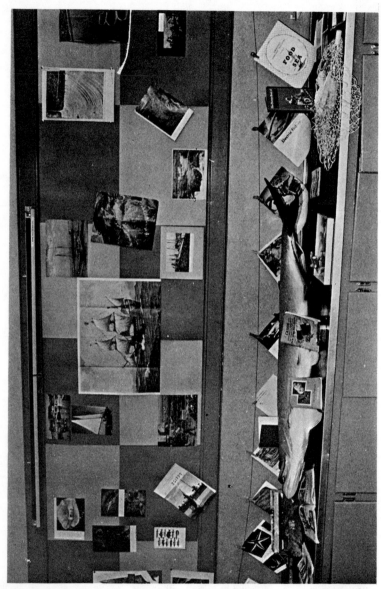

A well organized vertical file collection can provide a broad spectrum of varied types of interest-stimulating materials to dramatize major study units, such as in this fourth grade presentation of the FISHING INDUSTRY.

V
Processing
Tools

Since material begins to come in relatively soon after requests have been mailed, it is practical to have all of the processing equipment on hand at the very beginning.

The list of mounting tools, proposed below, consists of generally inexpensive equipment which is readily obtainable through regular stationery supply channels.

I The list (for legal size file materials):
> Mounting board: 14-point manilla oaktag sheets; cut 10" x 14½"
>
> Rubber cement and thinner; an adhesive "pick-up"; perforated adhesive cloth, 1"; staples
>
> Editors' shears; single-edge razor blade and sheath holder; paper cutter
>
> Steel-edge ruler; sharp #2 pencils; clear plastic triangle, at least 12"
>
> Red (and assorted colors) nylon-tip pens; roll-labels, manilla
>
> Broad work surface

II Optional equipment (for all sizes of material):
> Dry mount press
> Backing cloth
> Fixative spray
> Transparent plastic laminating sheets

III The list (for oversized file materials):
> Mounting Board: 200#, manilla oaktag; cut 24" x 36"

   T-square, 36″ long
   Double-sided adhesive tape
   Roll-labels, manilla
   Plain paper bags, 20″ x 16½″ (optional)

Mounting Stock

Mounting Board of 14-point manilla oaktag sheets appears to be the best weight. Stock much lighter than this has been found unable to withstand extensive handling. Experience proves that much heavier stock is too difficult for untrained artists to work with. Too, much heavier board has a tendency to warp. Most magazine pictures may be cropped to fit on this 10″ x 14½″ size with no important loss of detail. For larger pictures, two of these boards can be joined together on a hinge (*Figure 29*) without adding inconvenient thicknesses to the files. Conversely, the board can be cut in half to 10″ x 7¼″ (*Figure 30*) and still maintain a pleasant "frame" for the mounted picture.

Regardless of how small a picture is, the mount must *never* be smaller than half a full board, i.e., 10″ x 7¼″. There are two reasons for this:

1. Shorter boards are apt to get lost in the file when placed among taller pieces.

2. Subject headings on short boards can easily be obscured by taller material.

The alternate approach of filing shorter mounted pictures in file folders should be avoided. To begin with, usage has shown that uniformly mounted pictures, kept in individual picture sections, are used more frequently. Equally, if not more important, they also have a considerably longer life span than those which are scattered within various folders along with pamphlets and stapled articles. Finally, mounted pictures will add too much bulk to the file folders themselves thereby making them ungainly in appearance and unwieldy in use.

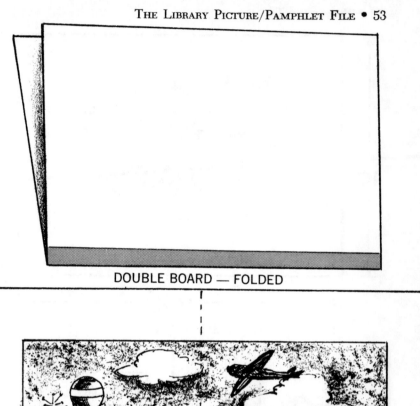

DOUBLE BOARD — FOLDED

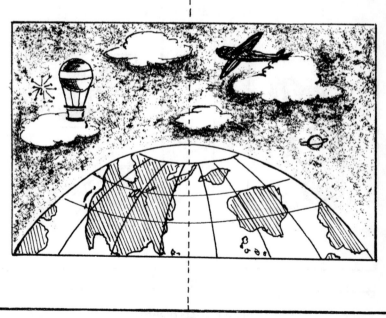

DOUBLE BOARD — OPEN

FIGURE 29

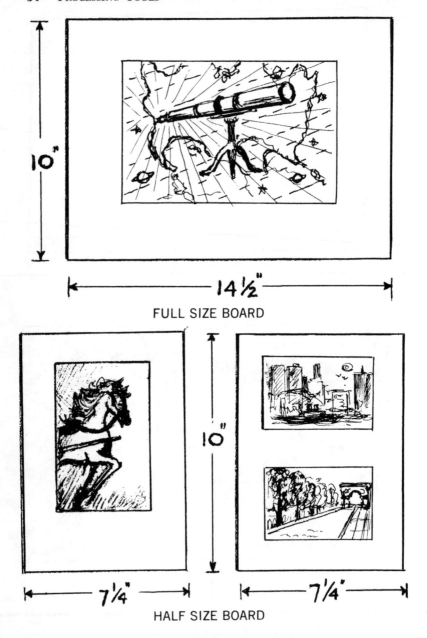

10"

14½"

FULL SIZE BOARD

10"

7¼"

7¼"

HALF SIZE BOARD

FIGURE 30

The neutral buff color unobtrusively enhances the material which it backs. Various strongly colored stocks which are offered for mounting purposes have a tendency to fade after a time. In addition, they cannot be re-used. This will be explained in greater detail on pages 66 and 67.

The quantity of mounting board ordered at one time depends upon how speedily the library staff works. This varies from year to year, but 1,000 sheets should be enough for a start.

Adhesive and Thinner

Rubber Cement is the cleanest adhesive with which to work. Since it will thicken on the shelf once the container has been opened, supplies must be ordered accordingly. Necessarily, the quantity needed will vary with each library. A normal elementary school library vertical file collection which emphasizes pictures uses an average of two one-gallon cans and four four-ounce containers (for individual use) per school year. Significantly larger amounts are required when starting a vertical file, but this also depends upon the speed with which the staff works. Thinner should be ordered at the same time so that the rubber cement may be kept fluid, as required. The supplier of school and library needs can be relied upon to recommend the best brand as well as to suggest the proper quantity specifically needed of each product.

Adhesive "Pick-Up"

An *adhesive "pick-up"* is made by allowing a spoonful of cement to dry on a non-porous surface so that it may be lifted, or peeled off in a wad. When rubbed along the cemented surfaces of the picture, the wad cleanly removes —or picks-up—any spots of dried rubber cement. It keeps indefinitely while growing in size with use. Although it turns black from exposure to air, this does not affect its performance. Despite the fact that it looks somewhat like an eraser and acts like one, it is *not* an eraser and must not be used as such.

Adhesive Cloth

Perforated Adhesive Cloth is used for creating one long yet foldable piece out of two mounting boards by hinging the backs of the long edges together (*Figure 29*). Cellophane tape is too fragile for this purpose and should not be used.

Staples

Staples are used for joining pages of *unmounted* articles. Stapling or taping pictures to the mounting surfaces is not recommended since stapled pictures tear easily when taken in and out of the files. In addition, the staples can cut busy, incautious fingers. Tape is costly, time consuming in application, and does not function as well as rubber cement when used for mounting purposes.

Cutting and Trimming Equipment

Editors' Shears are essential and should be treated with tender, loving care. *Do not use for anything but paper.* The worker will be doing an unbelievable amount of cutting (little of it intricate, however) and will need a scissors which fits comfortably balanced in her hand without strain. With the long, sharp, tapered blades of this type of shears, long, sharp, even sweeps are possible. When mounted, the picture thus presents a smoothly professional appearance. When one is preparing dozens of items at a sitting, such an effect is almost impossible to achieve or maintain with any other size or type of scissors. It is not worth economizing on this item.

A *razor blade and holder* may be preferred to a scissors. Blades are always necessary for neatly removing pages from a bound magazine which is to be kept for further use at a future date.

Hand-operated paper cutters, either for trimming individual pictures or for slicing mounting boards in half, are time savers, indeed. However, in time, all but the most expensive cutters tend to dull and become inaccurate. Unless someone is prepared to keep close watch on the blade, boards and pictures are bound to be marred by jagged, improperly measured edges. Since the blade is also affected by the shifting weights of paper and heavier mounting boards, two paper cutters are desirable: one for paper and one for board. Loss of display effectiveness is not worth the gain in time, so be sure that the paper cutter is a good one to start with and be sure that it is properly maintained.

Measuring Tools

The need for *rulers and sharp pencils* is self-evident. A *steel-edged ruler* is necessary for those times when no other tool will do for gauging a dimension, the steel-edge being used for a surface against which to guide a razor blade. Plastic or wooden rulers will be nicked by the blade and will be worthless after the first or second use.

The *plastic triangle* is an invaluable accessory for drawing straight trimming lines and for marking marginal areas with little effort and no measuring. It assures perfectly vertical, horizontal, or extended lines without having to constantly pick up and put down a ruler.

The actual manipulation of the triangle is as simple as using a ruler whose edge is the pencil's guide. First, decide just where the cutting lines are to be drawn on the page. Then, place one leg (edge) of the triangle against any straight line printed on the item. (Do not use the edge of the page since, despite all appearances, it is not straight. Its apparent "true" line is really an optical illusion.) If the chosen line is vertical, the other leg of the triangle will automatically provide the guide for drawing the horizontal trimming line. Similarly, if the leg is first placed against a horizontal line of the page, the second leg will be the guide for drawing the desired vertical line. The hypotenuse of the triangle can be used for drawing extended lines from those that are too short. Either illustrations or text can be used as a guide for the edges of the triangle.

All lines, drawn in pencil, will be cut away when the page is trimmed for mounting. The triangle should be of clear plastic which is not only comfortably light in weight but which also permits the artist to see all areas of the item being trimmed (*Figure 31*).

Labeling Equipment

Red pens and roll-labels will all be described in further detail in Chapters VI and VII.

Work Table

Broad work surface. An efficient job cannot be done, nor will the interest of the staff be maintained, if the work surface is cramped and skimpy. Almost all of the above mentioned equipment will have to be at hand when mounting material for the files. Otherwise, if the staff must continually interrupt its work to procure supplies, the job of processing becomes a wearisome burden. Tables used for this purpose should be able to withstand the solvents used in adhesives, possible nicks from sharp cutting tools, etc.

Dry Mount Press

Dry Mount Press. Where the budget permits, the library can take advantage of what is perhaps the most widely

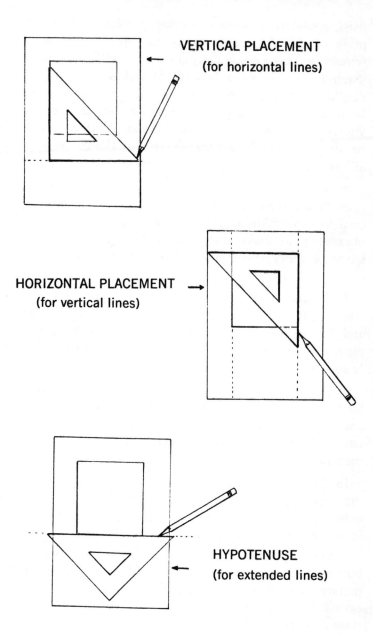

VERTICAL PLACEMENT
(for horizontal lines)

HORIZONTAL PLACEMENT
(for vertical lines)

HYPOTENUSE
(for extended lines)

FIGURE 31

used, commercial photo-mounting process: the dry mount press (*Figure 32*). The variety and sizes of flat materials which can be permanently mounted with this table-top machine are almost unlimited. Materials mounted with a dry mount press do not curl, peel, or warp due to age or to atmospheric changes. The machine can be operated by anyone after a simple demonstration and perfect results can be obtained even by novices. Naturally, the press supplants all other bonding materials and methods.

Because of its relatively high cost (in comparison to hand operations), the librarian must first decide if the type of vertical file collection will warrant such an expenditure. The librarian must make a serious analysis of the purpose and scope of the vertical file—and of whom it is intended to serve.

The ultimate functioning of the file and the material which it contains is directly related to the type of library and its patrons. Therefore, the extent of the need for permanently treated material will vary from library to library, from file to file.

In the school library, the collection may be valued more for the hard-core information it contains than for the rarity and esthetic appeal of its individual items. Hence, since the contents may be neither exceptional nor irreplaceable, permanency may not be a major factor for consideration.

In the small public library, which may also act as the archives for local documents, historical papers, antique maps, etc., permanency may be highly desirable despite the fact that the material may be infrequently used.

In the large public library, which caters to both private borrowers and commercially oriented users, thousands of pictures may have to be mounted permanently (on rigid, extremely heavy stock) to withstand the pressures of constant demand and heavy traffic.

The religious library is in much the same position as the

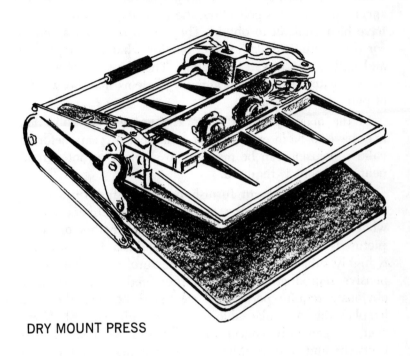

DRY MOUNT PRESS

TACKING IRON

FIGURE 32

small public library with an added factor: because of the special nature of its collection, the majority of its items may have been difficult to obtain. They are prized, not so much for their actual "dollar" value, but for what they represent and add to the private collection. Therefore, a proportionately greater than normal amount of items may be worthy of permanent treatment.

In the majority of instances, the vertical file collection may have to be in existence for a number of years before a valid conclusion can be made as to whether or not permanent treatment is required.

It is not possible to furnish hard and fast rules as to what is or is not worthy of permanent treatment nor to what represents "expensive" equipment. Whether or not a picture is "irreplaceable" or "expendable" is a decision which is highly subjective, at times. To be sure, a number of expensive reproductions, rare pictures, and documents may obviously require permanent treatment because they are irreplaceable or replaceable only at prohibitive cost. However, as generally conceived, a vertical file collection is transient and flexible. Most of its contents, therefore, are considered to be largely expendable.

The life-span of the "average" (temporary or semi-permanent) mounted picture in the "average" library has been estimated to be approximately ten years. This figure can be less than one year for an item in heavy demand in an elementary school and as high as twenty years (or more) in a university or private library for highly desirable, but infrequently used items. For the average school and small library, it may be more important to have a larger collection of timely material on temporary mounts than to have funds immobilized in expensive equipment.

School libraries, however, may very well be able to afford a dry mount press or other costly equipment if such units are made available to all the schools at some central location, or if an audio-visual aids center is available to supervise the use, preparation and distribution of these materials throughout the school system.

In considering permanent treatment of flat material, three further details might be examined: the first deals with backing; the second, with surface treatment; the third, with overall protection of the material. In each of the three instances the librarian again must weigh the value and the life expectancy of the item against the expenditure of time and/or funds.

Backing Cloth

Backing Cloth. There may be certain fairly large items (pictorial, map, graph, etc.) in any vertical file collection which definitely require durable yet flexible backings. In such cases, it is suggested that a cloth backing of waxed cambric, unbleached muslin, or cheesecloth be used. For detailed, precise instructions on how to apply cloth backings, see Margaret Rufsvold's *Audio-Visual School Library Service.*[1] Another type of backing cloth, which is applied either with a dry mount press or a household iron, is available through commercial sources. It is much cleaner and considerably easier to use than the above.

Fixative Spray

Fixative Spray may be applied to the surfaces of all mounted pictures to protect them somewhat from fingerprints, dust, etc. Full directions for application are printed on the labels of each can. While this has not proved absolutely essential, it is worth considering. The cost is negligible, but it can be a time-consuming process.

Transparent Plastic Coverings and Laminations

Transparent Coverings and Laminating Sheets are avail-

---

[1] Margaret I. Rufsvold, *Audio-Visual School Library Service,* Chicago, American Library Association, 1949, p. 66.

able in thin gauge plastics with pressure sensitive adhesive backing. Some, applied to the front surface of a picture, act as protective coverings. Others, applied to both front and back (thus forming a plastic "sandwich"), shield the entire unit from wear. The various plastic films which are suited to vertical file use do require a mastery of differing styles of application. However, most methods are quite simple to learn. Clear, illustrated directions for general application procedures are given in *The Practical Audio-Visual Handbook for Teachers* by Herbert E. Scuorzo.[1] One caution is necessary: in the majority of cases, the adhesive bonds instantly. Therefore, care must be taken in placing the plastic film on the material which is to be covered or laminated. Heavier, semi-rigid laminations must be sent to professional plastic laminators.

Since many adhesives and plastic films tend to yellow or dry and crack over extended periods of time, it is essential that the librarian investigate this "aging" factor. Inquiries should be addressed directly to the manufacturer.

Whether commercially processed or applied by the library staff, protective plastic covering can prove to be a relatively costly procedure if done on a broad scale. Furthermore, it should be realized that each layer of plastic film may add significant thickness to each treated item. Where housing and space are likely to be a problem, this is an aspect well worth considering before a decision is made to treat material in this manner.

Generally, laminating or covering vertical file material does not seem to be necessary, but the librarian should familiarize herself with its possibilities for particularly rare or delicate pieces in the collection.

Mounting supplies for oversized file items are discussed in Chapter IX.

---

[1] Herbert E. Scuorzo, *The Practical Audio-Visual Handbook for Teachers*, West Nyack, New York, Parker Publishing Company, Inc., 1967, p. 178.

VI

Mechanics of Processing
Pictures and Pamphlets

Mounting Pictures

With the staff all set and the criteria (INTEREST, IN-TEGRITY, IMAGINATION, IMMEDIACY) in mind, all is ready for processing. Strive to get as many pictures as possible mounted on individual boards since a flat picture is more versatile than one that is part of a brochure or article. *If it's worth saving, it's worth mounting.* There are several good reasons for this concept, although some may not be as obvious as others. Usage has proved that:

1. Illustrations contained within the stapled pages of a mainly textual article do not have the display value and the mobility of individual pieces.

2. The borrower's selection of desired pictures must not be hampered by what is contained within the article itself.

3. With separate mounting, there are no distracting elements surrounding the picture detracting from its dramatic, pleasant effect.

4. An unmounted picture, on fragile book or magazine stock, cannot withstand extensive handling. Even those visual aids which are printed on comparatively heavy paper (such as small posters and charts) will fray with continual usage.

5. A montage can be artfully created from several small, related pictures—the imaginative skill of the "paste-up" artist is the only limitation.

Occasionally, there may be a portion of a picture or caption that will extend a mere trifle beyond the board area.

Since it is such a very small detail, the inclination is to create a hinge or "flap", the theory being that one is saving another, entire board. However, it is far better to hinge on a second full mount because little flying flaps rip off in no time, no matter how carefully and attractively hinged. In no case should the material which is to be mounted extend to the full size of the mounting surface since the edges then tear or fray from wear no matter how carefully adhered to the board.

The oaktag serves as backing and as frame for all pictures. This approach is both labor- and dollar-saving for the staff since there is no need to cut and apply additional sheets of paper to frame each picture. Certainly, it greatly simplifies the whole process. It is not difficult to attractively arrange items on the mounts themselves. In addition, the uniform appearance thus created among all pictures in the collection is aesthetically satisfying.

Do not economize in spreading the rubber cement. All edges of every cut item should be fully and securely cemented. If the adhesive is merely dabbed at the corners, the loose sides rapidly tear when taken in and out of the file drawers. Use the "temporary mount" technique: it is permanent enough. Apply rubber cement to one surface only so that, if the picture must be removed at some future date, it can readily be peeled from the board. The backing can thus be used again. When rubber cement is applied to both picture and mounting surfaces, application is permanent and the board is destroyed when one attempts to remove the picture. If a fresh picture is subsequently pasted over an obsolete one, too much thickness is added to the board, and thus unnecessary thickness is added to the file itself. Since flexibility of material is the essence of the vertical file collection, pictures are frequently taken out of circulation for one reason or another: either they have become worn and unattractive or superior ones have been found on the same subject. However, the board still retains much of its freshness and since there are no frames or faded areas to worry about, the mount is usable once more.

When joining two boards together in order to create a double-sized mount (*Figure 29*), always apply the strip of adhesive cloth to the boards while they are in closed position. If applied with the boards open, there is no allowance for "spread" and the tape will pull off the mount the first time the boards are folded together.

Pictures which are purchased through commercial sources are usually on heavy stock which requires no further processing.

Mounting Photographs

When mounting photographs of either glossy or matte finish, the "permanent mount" technique is the only method which will successfully mate the photograph to the mount without subsequent lifting. The following method is most satisfactory when working with rubber cement:

a) Apply a light, even coating of adhesive to the entire back of the picture surface and to the entire area which it will cover of the mount. Be extremely cautious in application because an excess of the solvents in the adhesive can adversely affect the emulsion of the print. In addition, since rubber cements are highly flammable in the liquid form, the workroom must be well ventilated.

b) Expose adhesive coated surfaces to the air until dry (tacky to the touch, but not wet). At this stage, the two coated surfaces will form a firm bond instantly upon contact. In view of this, care should be taken to insure proper positioning *before* mating the surfaces.

c) Cover the face of the photograph with wax paper when preparing to flatten it to the mount surface.

d) To ensure a satisfactory bond, firmly roll an ordinary rolling pin back and forth over the wax paper.

For explicit and detailed directions in the proper use of a "dry mount press", consult the literature that is supplied with each machine.

Display Accessories

At this stage of the operations, the librarian may wish to investigate the numerous accessories available for affixing prepared material to bulletin boards.[1] Thumb tacks may be employed provided that they are used to "frame" the picture rather than to pierce it. Insert the shank of the tack tangent to the mounting board with the heads of the tacks overlapping and supporting the face of the picture (*Figure 33*). Far more attractive, are ¼" nails which are placed in the same manner as are thumbtacks. The tiny heads are virtually invisible and do not detract from the display in any way.

Perhaps the librarian will feel that the additional time and expense involved in applying more complicated devices than thumb tacks or wire nails is unnecessary. Nevertheless, the librarian should examine these various alternatives in order to decide whether or not such display aids might be more convenient or otherwise desirable.

Captions for Mounted Materials

Captions, left unmounted, frequently go astray no matter how one tries to be careful. Captions must be mounted at the very same time the pictures are. In addition, if the material has any topical interest, a brief note of the date of the picture is necessary. As the vertical file collection grows both in size and in age, many an otherwise worthwhile piece will have to be discarded because of lack of accurate indications of time and place.

---

[1] Edgar Dale, *Audio-Visual Methods in Teaching*, Revised Edition, New York, Dryden Press, 1954, p. 257.

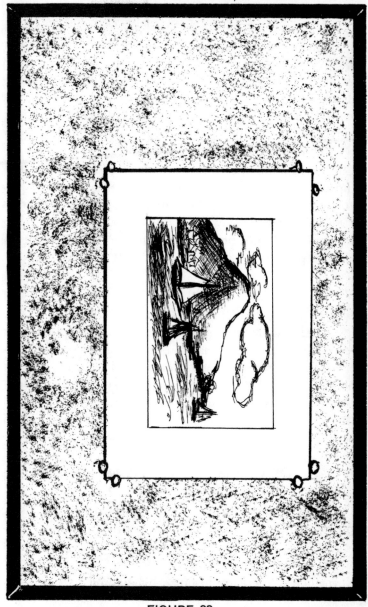

FIGURE 33

FULL SIZE PICTURE BOARD ON BULLETIN BOARD

(note thumb tack supports)

When processing copy from newspapers and magazines, also include the source name. Date, source, and caption usually can be typed on the roll-label along with the subject heading (*Figure* 38). If space is lacking on the label, a second label may be added in an appropriate place on the mounted picture. Sometimes, a penned notation is sufficient. In any case, it is important that this information is readily accessible to the viewer of the material.

Captions should *always* be affixed to the front of the unit. Although teachers often use pictures with an opaque projector or hold them up to the class as they lecture, pictures are just as often displayed on bulletin boards, walls, etc., thus requiring *frontal* access to *all* information regarding the displayed picture.

Picture Sets

Sets, or series, of pictures are treated in much the same way as individual items are with this one exception: sets received from a commercial source probably need no further attention from the layout artist. If the pieces are not already numbered for sequence and marked with appropriate subject headings, do so in the standard manner. The set is then placed in a file jacket (see page 102). Visibly and strongly worded on the face of the jacket should be the notation:

SET OF (number of) PICTURES.
PLEASE KEEP TOGETHER.

There are comparatively few instances when the "set" approach must be created from separately gathered pictures. Keeping the file as simple as possible is a fundamental concept. Sets tend to add just one more factor of complexity.

Nevertheless, there are instances when only a set will suffice:

1. A number of closely inter-related pictures might be found in a magazine essay; or,

2. A large amount of very small pictures (such as are found in popular regional date books).

In the former case, the pictures are processed as usual and a file jacket supplied. In the latter situation, if the librarian decides it is not necessary to mount the pictures individually, they are enveloped in a jacket as a set. Each picture, however, should still be separately labeled (*Figure 16*).

File jackets are always placed *within* the file folders.

Pamphlets and Articles: Subject Headings

Pamphlets, multi-paged articles, and unmounted pictures are relatively quick and easy to process.

Subject headings are printed in clear, legible red on the outside cover or on the first page where they can be readily identified. Red is a good color to use for the headings because it generally shows up on most backgrounds. However, any strong vibrant color will do—just as long as it is consistently used for this particular job. Fine line, (bamboo, plastic, or nylon tip) pens are ideal. Two precautions which should be noted about such pens are (1) they must be kept *tightly* covered when not in use to avoid drying, and (2) when writing with them, heavy hand-pressure will swiftly blunt the fine writing points.

Often, the color of the pamphlet cover is such that no color for identifying subject headings can be seen satisfactorily. In these instances, a snip of the scissors, diagonally across the cover, will expose a white or light colored page below. The subject heading can then be printed directly on this second layer (*Figure 34*).

Occasionally, even this method will prove unsuitable. Therefore, a roll-label, affixed to the cover, will furnish an adequate face on which to print the subject heading (*Figure 34*).

A standard location for the pamphlet heading should be

FIGURE 34   PAMPHLETS: Location of Subject Headings

Pamphlet In Reading Position
(Subject Heading: upper right side)

PAMPHLETS IN FILE FOLDER

FIGURE 35

established so that there is minimum delay in identifying the needed items. The upper right-hand corner has been found to be generally serviceable since the majority of such pieces are put into the file long-side-horizontal thereby placing this corner at the upper-left. The right-hand corner is then uppermost in the file folder (*Figure 35*). On smaller items, the subject headings should be printed across the tops because these pieces are placed in an upright position in the folders. It is important to mention, however, that the actual location of the subject headings on the pamphlets is not as important as is the fact that, once selected, the location should be consistently used on all printed matter which is not mounted. When twenty or more pieces are selected from, or returned to, the vertical file, there simply isn't time to hunt for and decipher erratic identifications.

Pamphlets and Articles: Date Notations

For future reference, the date the pamphlet was received should also be noted in an easily and quickly seen spot on or within the item. Since the date of reception is often quite different from the date the pamphlet was published, the notation proves helpful should the timeliness of the data be in question or should there be a need to re-order. If desired, the date on which the item is likely to be discarded from the file may also be noted on the cover. This will facilitate periodic weeding of the file.

For libraries in which the distinction is made, all pamphlets, articles, clippings, etc., should be marked (either in pencil or with a rubber stamp) "reference" or "lending."

When selecting articles from magazines, always re-check to be certain that all of the feature is removed.

Frequently, when working rapidly and with a large amount of different items, the fact that the desired article is continued on one or more successive pages can easily be overlooked. Magazine articles, often surrounded by advertising columns, should be trimmed of all potentially confusing, extraneous details. If this is not possible, unwanted features should be blocked out with a few, firm strokes (or an "X") of a broad tip, felt marker. Multi-paged articles should be stapled and, wherever possible, folded so that their titles are uppermost and are plainly visible.

Clippings

As noted previously, fragile newspaper clippings which are of lasting interest should be mounted or laminated (see pages 29, 63-64). However, most news items which are of topical and of current interest may be put into file folders without further processing. (The subject heading, source, date of item, and library identification must appear on each clipping.) Clippings have a comparatively short life when not further prepared which is quite satisfactory for this type of material.

However, some librarians may prefer preserving their clippings a bit longer. In such instances, it is possible to fashion small folders especially for clippings. A standard file folder is cut to size; the clipping is pasted to the inside, right-hand leaf. Subject heading and ownership are placed on the outside, top of the folder (*Figure 36*). Subject heading, source, date of item, and ownership are placed on the clipping itself for added identification (*Figure 36*). When the clipping is withdrawn from the file, the folder also is discarded.

While it is true that this method lengthens the life of a clipping, it is extremely doubtful whether such a rapidly obsolescent item merits the time and the expense of such preparation.

Processing oversized material is discussed in Chapter IX.

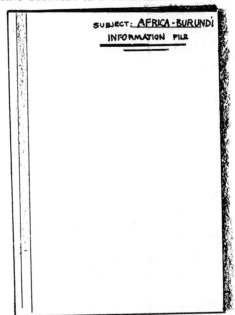

CLIPPING FOLDER—CLOSED

CLIPPING FOLDER—OPEN

FIGURE 36

VII

Assigning Subject Headings and Labeling

Assigning subject headings to vertical file material is an important professional job—even more exacting than it is with books. In cataloging books, the librarian has the help of an accepted, standardized classification system; with vertical file materials, she has only a broad, loose alphabetical arrangement with which to work. In addition, the librarian must employ numerous cross references for vertical file material in order to alert the user to subject divisions and to related subjects.

Subject Headings

Subject headings in the vertical file should be the same as those used for books. This ensures uniformity in the card catalog and guarantees that users will not miss vertical file materials. (*Sears List of Subject Headings*[1] is recommended as the primary source for school and small public libraries.)

Within the Dewey Decimal Classification System, the broad category of GEOLOGY is given the number 550; the divisions of this subject are given numbers 551.2 (for volcanoes), 551.43 (for mountains), 551.45 (for deserts), 551.46 (for oceans), etc. Thus the borrower need go to only one section of the library for books on all these related subjects.

In the vertical file, on the other hand, *each subject should be treated individually rather than as a subdivision of a broader subject heading.* Since the four subjects, DESERTS, MOUNTAINS, OCEAN, VOLCANOES, for example, are then found in four different locations within the file cabinet, cross references must be used—both in the vertical file and in the card catalog:

GEOLOGY

see also

DESERTS

MOUNTAINS

OCEAN

VOLCANOES

Additionally, in this example, each of these subjects will probably contain cross references to GEOLOGY.

The use of broad subject headings with subdivisions is possible in the vertical file. For example "GEOLOGY – DESERTS" and "GEOLOGY–VOLCANOES" would bring related materials together in the file. However, this method is *not* recommended since the user tends to think in terms of the specific subject wanted: "DESERTS" and "VOLCANOES."

Whichever way is adopted—specific subject headings with cross references or broad categories with subdivisions—the card catalog should clearly lead the user to the desired subject.

At first, it may seem better for school librarians to use the individual study units for each grade as guides for subject headings. However, this system leads to complications for other grades since ideas are never limited to one age level or one group.

Because children begin learning library practice early in their school careers, subject headings need not be altered to fit the terminology and the vocabulary of each grade level: children can handle ZOOLOGICAL GARDENS with almost as much facility as they do ZOOS. Furthermore, it is healthy library practice to accustom children to that which they will have to work with in other libraries. To repeat, when there is an alternative in selecting the proper subject

---

[1] Minnie E. Sears, *Sears List of Subject Headings*, 9th edition, edited by Barbara Marietta Westby, New York, H. W. Wilson Company, 1965.

heading, work toward the highest vocabulary level. It is essential, however, that numerous "see" references be made from familiar words in the child's vocabulary to the sometimes less known subject headings.

Despite close adherence to the major subject headings, subdivisions, and cross references found in *Sears*, additional headings are sometimes needed. For instance, in 1956, AEROSPACE and ASTRONAUTICS were not standard subject headings. Today, not only are these subjects used, but related subject headings are numerous. For example:

AEROSPACE	GUIDED MISSILES
ARTIFICIAL SATELLITES	OUTER SPACE
ASTRONAUTICS	SPACE FLIGHT
ASTRONAUTS	SPACE MEDICINE

Included in these major subject headings are additional references to CAPE KENNEDY, TELSTAR, and many others. AEROSPACE first appeared as a subject heading in *Readers' Guide to Periodical Literature* in 1963. Since then, it has appeared often under such specific headings as AEROSPACE INDUSTRIES, AEROSPACE CORPORATION, etc. It does not appear in *Webster's Third New International Dictionary*, unabridged, published by Merriam-Webster in 1962. It does appear in their abridged edition for 1965. Probably the word had not yet come into common use when that section was prepared in the unabridged, 1962 edition. The *World Book Encyclopedia Dictionary*, published in 1965, gives a definition of the word, AEROSPACE, and also quotes from the *Manchester Guardian*, as follows:

> Aeronautics . . . is giving place to a
> wide extension in what is coming to
> be known as the 'aerospace sciences.'

The subject appears in *Compton's Pictured Encyclopedia* for the first time in 1965. Martin Caidin, in his *Man-in-Space Dictionary*[1] defines AEROSPACE as "a term that came into

---

[1] Caidin, Martin, *Man-in-Space Dictionary*, New York, Dutton, 1963, p. 13.

common usage by 1960." The above research is more than sufficient to give support to AEROSPACE as a valid subject heading in the vertical file.

As a general principle, it is unwise to adopt headings not found in established subject heading tools. Occasionally, when working with extremely current materials it becomes necessary (as in the example above). In such cases, it is advisable to enter the new subject heading with the word "tentative" after it in the authoritative subject headings list which is being used by the librarian. When an authority for this use is found, the "tentative" is erased and the name of the authority put in its place.

.Sometimes, a more satisfactory heading will be found than the one which is in use. In this instance, the tentative heading should be erased altogether and the new subject heading entered instead. All vertical file materials and cards in the catalog will then have to be changed accordingly.

In the search for subject headings, encyclopedias, dictionaries, and all other standard reference works are practical aids which may be used to supplement the librarian's professional guides. *Readers' Guide to Periodical Literature* is especially helpful in this area because it has current topics. Since borrowers work with the above sources, it is essential that subjects come within a familiar frame of reference.

Frequently, a picture or a pamphlet seems exclusively suited to but one subject. After processing, other possibilities become apparent. The solution may lie in a "see also" reference (as illustrated in *Figure 37*). It is also a common experience to find an item which is obviously important and most worthy, yet which eludes precise classification. In school libraries, a discussion with the instructor likely to teach this subject is often helpful. His suggestions usually are all that are needed to indicate the proper direction. Final decisions will have to depend upon the current requirements of individual libraries.

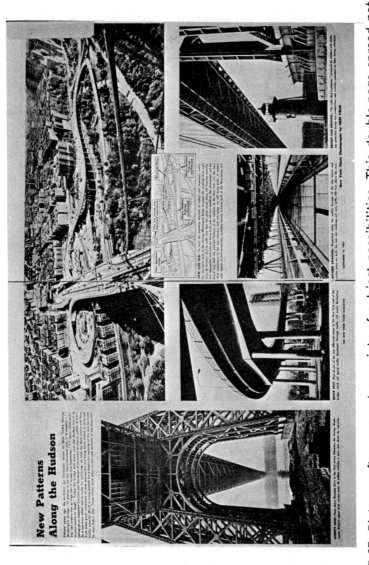

FIGURE 37: Pictures often present a variety of subject possibilities. This double-page spread not only is useful for the study of BRIDGES, but also for the study of NEW YORK—NEW JERSEY (metropolitan area), NEW YORK—NEW YORK CITY, RIVERS, NEW YORK (state), ROADS, TRANSPORTATION, and LIGHTHOUSES.

© 1963 by The New York Times Company. Reprinted by permission.

"Authority" File

It is most important that a record be kept of all subjects used in the vertical file and of all cross references made in the card catalog in order to ensure that uniform headings are assigned to like subjects. If there is no organized control, when new material is to be added, the librarian and her staff often will have to spend precious time in checking through the files to ascertain which subject headings have been previously employed.

A simple and effective method of establishing such a system is merely to check (in pencil) the appropriate entry in the subject heading book being used by the librarian and to write in any added headings. A colored pencil can be used for vertical file materials to easily differentiate them from the subject entries of books which may have been entered in the same fashion.

Another approach which may be employed is to put the subject headings and cross references on individual cards thus creating an "authority" file for the vertical file collection. However, checking the subject heading book is preferred to this method since a card file takes substantially more clerical time.

A third alternative is to keep a typewritten list of the subject headings. However, this is not very satisfactory since it is difficult to space the entries so that headings and cross references can be added in proper alphabetical order. A loose leaf notebook, with a separate page (or pages) for each letter, is preferred to straight lists although it does not entirely solve the problem.

Labeling Mounted Pictures

Once subject headings have been assigned, labels must be typed for mounted materials. The main subject heading is typed on the manilla-colored roll-label in CAPITAL LETTERS (*Figure* 38):

AFRICA — ANIMALS
"Game Preserve; Kenya, 1961"
(Life Magazine)

FIGURE 38

This label is affixed to the mounted picture in *one place only*—the upper, left-hand corner in the to-be-filed position—regardless of how the mount may ultimately be displayed (*Figure 39*). (At times, part of the label may interfere with important caption details; it takes no time to trim the label to fit.)

This position is the least disturbing spot on the picture when it is displayed, yet the most conspicuous and convenient in the file. Since the manilla color matches the mount, its neat and innocuous appearance does not interfere with the displayed picture.

Unmounted pictures are treated as are the pamphlets and articles (see pages 71-75).

Occasionally, subject headings may have to be placed on the backs of unmounted pictures. In such instances, the subject heading can be hand-printed directly on the item instead of typed on a roll-label. Nylon or bamboo tip pens are ideal; broad tip, felt markers, on the other hand, must be used with extreme care since they may "bleed" through to the front surface.

Still, some may feel that the label on the front of the picture does mar its display effectiveness. It is quite possible to place the subject heading on the back of the picture. However, it is both more difficult to locate specific pictures in the files and to replace them when subject headings are on the backs. Also, there is some educational value in looking at displayed pictures when the subject headings the librarian has assigned to them are visible to the viewer.

Card Catalog

Just as all books in the library are cataloged, so should all vertical file material be cataloged. However, this is a much simpler process than it is for books since the librarian works with subjects only, *not with individual items.* The latter are too numerous and too ephemeral to warrant separate cards for each piece.

CATALOG CARDS: COLOR-BANDED

A color-banded catalog card should be used to designate vertical file materials so that the borrower can easily identify these resources in the card catalog. (If, for some reason, printed color-banded cards are not available, they can be created by drawing a band with a broad tip, felt pen across the top of a white catalog card.)

In 1962, the Public and School Library Services Bureau of the New Jersey State Library joined with the Audio-Visual Office of the Division of Curriculum and Instruction in recommending color-banded catalog cards for instructional materials. At that time, although films, phonograph records, etc., were given specific color designations, no reference was made to the vertical file. Since the color blue was not then assigned to any particular audio-visual tool, it was decided (locally) to use blue for the vertical file. Therefore, unless it comes in conflict with prevailing practice, blue can be used as the standard vertical file color.

Many librarians use colored cards in the catalog for non-book materials. Whichever method or color is adopted by the librarian, color is preferred in contrast to the standard white which is used for books.

CATALOG CARDS: CALL NUMBER POSITION

In addition to the color of the card, it is suggested that "vertical file" be stamped on each card in the upper left-hand corner where the call number is usually placed. Although this isn't totally necessary, it does help to further

HALF SIZE

VERTICAL

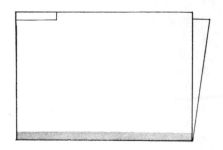

DOUBLE BOARD

FULL SIZE
HORIZONTAL

FULL SIZE
VERTICAL

HALF SIZE
HORIZONTAL

FIGURE 39

emphasize the nature of the materials. This is especially helpful in elementary school libraries where children are taught library skills.

If "oversized file" and/or "x-ray file" materials also are available for the subject, rubber stamps to this effect should be placed immediately below the vertical file imprint.

In school libraries, the "PROF." (professional) designation does not need to appear on the catalog card. However, this notation may be made on the file folder so that the librarian or the teacher is alerted to the fact that "PROF." material, for the subject, is available.

CATALOG CARDS: FORM

Catalog cards for the vertical file collection can follow the standard format used for books:

1. The subject heading is typed two lines below the color band and twelve spaces in from the left-hand side of the card (*Figure 40*).

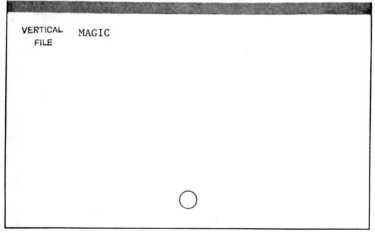

VERTICAL   MAGIC
    FILE

FIGURE 40

2. Where applicable, the words "see" or "see also" are typed two lines below the subject heading and fourteen spaces in from the left-hand side of the card.

3. The subject headings which are referred to are typed two lines below the "see" or "see also" references and ten spaces in from the left-hand side of the card (*Figure 41*).

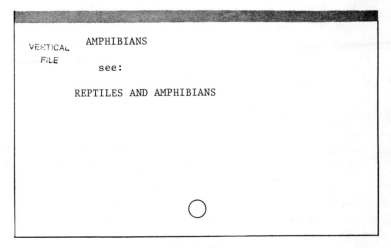

FIGURE 41

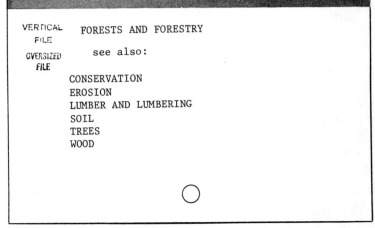

FIGURE 42

When two or more subject headings are listed as references, they are typed in a column and in alphabetical order (*Figure 42*).

All subject headings are typed in upper case letters.
No punctuation is used.

CATALOG CARDS: CROSS REFERENCES

Standard library practice puts all cross references on individual subject cards. However, there is some merit in using one card for all references when treating vertical file materials. Since each subject can relate to several different individual items within several different subject headings, and since many cross references are desirable for subjects in the vertical file collection, putting all references on one card seems to be easier for the borrowers to use. Certainly, by adopting this system, significant space is saved in the card catalog. Not the least consideration is the fact that much clerical time is saved by typing one card instead of numerous collateral reference cards, as often is the case.

In elementary school libraries, children can be taught that this system only applies to vertical file materials: with all the pertinent data on catalog cards for books, there would not be room for such a practice to be attempted. Furthermore, catalog cards for books deal with one book, one title only, and the need for "see" and "see also" references does not appear to be as great as it does for vertical file materials. At this time, this approach is in an experimental stage, but it does seem to work quite well. It does not appear to have caused confusion or poor library orientation among the youngsters with whom it has been tried.

CATALOG CARDS: FILING

In a school library, it is advantageous to file cards for book and non-book materials in the card catalog. A teacher or a pupil, looking for a specific subject, may not know in advance how he is to present or to study the subject. Since all related material is concentrated in one section of the card catalog, he can determine just what kinds of materials are available to him. These may well be pictures, pamphlets, film strips, tapes, and phono discs in addition to books and standard reference works. Moreover, the simple discovery of a diversity of media, in itself, often leads to exciting innovations in presentation of subject matter and a dynamic new approach to learning.

FIGURE 43: Vertical File material is cataloged as are all other library reference resources.

No specific order for filing these non-book materials has yet been established. An alphabetical order may be used: books, films, filmstrips, phonograph records, realia, slides, tapes, transparencies, and vertical file. One recommended arrangement is to file the cards in order of frequency of use: books, vertical file, film strips, slides, phono discs, transparencies, films, tapes, realia. As the various collections of non-book materials develop, one or the other may begin to show more demand than was evidenced at first. In such instances, it is not necessary for the librarian to revise the order of the catalog cards. Once a definite system has been established within the individual library, it is best to continue it. It does not matter, at this point, just what system is used in filing these various cards within the catalog just as long as an order is established and is followed consistently by the individual library.

It is important that all subjects, regardless of type of material, are filed in strict alphabetical order within the catalog. In order to maintain consistency of filing procedures and to ensure maximum ease of usage, it once more is stressed that an accepted subject heading list be followed.

Ownership

At this point, processed material is almost ready for filing and for circulation. Just one more step remains. *All* vertical file material must be marked for ownership because it can so easily go astray. Whatever system the individual library uses for identification, also should be employed for the vertical file collection. *The librarian should see to it that every piece is properly identified since this is the library's only mark of ownership.* It is suggested that pictures, whether mounted or unmounted, be stamped on the backs in order to preserve their appearances. Clippings and single-page items may be stamped on the fronts. Pamphlets should be identified in several places (as are books).

VIII

Housing and Maintaining

the Vertical File Collection

The time has come when all is prepared and ready for filing.

It is strongly recommended that librarians consider housing both mounted pictures and pamphlets in one file cabinet. Considerable time is saved—for librarian, library staff, and library patron—by adopting this practice. Not only are materials on one specific subject easier to locate when in one place, but also filing, cataloging, and circulation procedures are greatly expedited.

The decision now has to be made as to what kind of housing (and filing system) is to be purchased by the librarian.

Selection Criteria

As information retrieval technology expands, new materials (and new applications for old materials) are developing which make a variety of housing/filing systems possible. The librarian, faced with numerous housing methods from which to choose, needs to consider several factors before making a final decision:

1. How much space (floor and wall; height, depth and width) is now available for housing? How much can be made available should additional units become necessary?

2. In the event that the library is renovated (for general modernization, expansion, etc.), can the housing be easily rearranged without undue reinstallation and labor costs?

3. Can additional units be added conveniently to accommodate normal vertical file expansion?

4. Is the housing securely based or installed to eliminate danger of tipping under the weight of its contents? Is it sturdy enough to withstand years of daily, constant use?

5. Does the filing system easily accommodate the wide disparity in sizes and in weights of vertical file items? Does it offer maximum protection for all pieces?

6. Can filed material be referred to *within* the housing itself—without wasted motion? Can the subject matter be readily scanned without having to be removed? Can it be identified quickly within its folder?

7. Can material be filed and removed easily? Is there a flat surface on which to place material, keeping both hands free for further work in the file?

8. Are unusual filing aids required which will add to basic costs? Are necessary filing aids quickly available locally when needed?

9. Is the filing system, itself, easily understandable to all potential users? Where applicable, can children make use of the system without lengthy instructions?

Occasionally, the librarian may have to compromise on one desirable feature in order to achieve another. The problem of selection often will be one of space limitations rather than one of expense.

If the librarian is considering housings and filing systems that deviate from the standard file cabinet, it is essential that she visit other libraries (and business offices) to determine exactly which system is best suited to her needs.

The most convenient housing is the familiar, standard, file cabinet.

File Cabinets

Do not submit a request for less than the best when submitting a requisition for a file cabinet—if necessary, it is possible to work from cardboard cartons until the budget can accommodate the real thing. It cannot be over-emphasized, at this juncture, how very much use (and abuse) the cabinets get if the material is properly selected and systematized. The files must be equal to the task. To stint here, at this crucial point, is false economy. Sturdy, steel files have many attributes: their drawers roll smoothly on roller bearings; their construction is rugged enough to withstand years of constant activity; their finish is impact- and scuff-proof. While their initial cost is not low, they are the least expensive over a period of years.

Of course, there are numerous different sizes and types of steel files on the market, but only four are of major interest to the librarian establishing a vertical file collection.

Legal Size Cabinet

The *legal size file* is probably the mainstay of picture/pamphlet collections—the vertical file collection. The legal size file (17½" wide x 26" deep; four-drawer) should have "swing front" drawers (as opposed to rigid fronts) which allow more load in a given space: the material can be tight when the drawer is closed, but loosens for easy access when open. An added factor, but worthwhile, is the inclusion of several metal dividers, or "follower blocks", within each file drawer. They are valuable in keeping the folders and mounted material neatly in place, erect without overcrowding; in preventing subdivisions from becoming bulky and unwieldy. Consequently, not only are filing and refiling made simpler but the pictures, themselves, are less easily damaged and torn by being forced into jammed sections.

Just as the legal size file is an essential element of every vertical file collection, so, too, is some sort of cabinet or system in which to house oversized materials, i.e., extra-large posters, maps, charts, and so forth. Housing for oversized is discussed in detail in Chapter IX.

X-Ray Cabinet

The third size file, *x-ray* or *large forms file* (21″ x 26½″), also should be considered at this time. So many large pictures are now being commercially produced, it has proven advantageous to have a file which is sized between legal and oversized. If it is decided to house pictures separately from pamphlets, these could be housed in the middle-size file while the legal size cabinet would be adequate for pamphlets.

Card Cabinet

A fourth size file, which may prove useful in the larger library, is the *card cabinet* (4″ x 6″ recommended; larger post cards may be filed in the main vertical file) which is used to house picture post cards exclusively. Post cards are not only good sources for scenic subjects, but excellent for details of architectural and fine art subjects. Because of its compact dimensions, this file sits conveniently on top of other cabinets and shelves presenting little problem for the space-hungry library. In addition, as the post card collection grows, necessitating additional drawers, this particular file can be stacked easily, interlocking one drawer upon the other. However, the usefulness of such files in school and small public libraries is questionable.

File Folders and Envelopes

Just as there are several types of file cabinets to be considered, so too are there several styles of file folders and envelopes from which to choose. There are three which are admirably suited to vertical file needs. All, it should be noted, must be the proper size for the file—whether it be legal, x-ray, or other—whether it be purchased or created by the library staff.

The most common file folder, and the least expensive in initial cash outlay, is perfectly serviceable. Folders of 11-point weight will be adequate for the general vertical file. The projecting tab definitely should be reinforced and of heavy weight. Center-cut is recommended because it permits quick reading of the off-centered labels on the mounted materials behind (*Figure 44*).

A second approach which some librarians may prefer is to put loose material (clippings, pamphlets, unmounted pictures, etc.) in *open-top* expansion file-envelopes. The open top is suggested so that the contents may be readily seen without having to remove the envelope from the file drawer; the accordion sides of the envelope expand to accommodate more material than can be contained by the usual file folder; the closed sides are an assurance that the contents will not fall out when envelopes are removed from the file cabinet. Colored plastic index tabs, pasted along the tops of the envelopes, help to locate subjects easily (*Figure 45*). Furthermore, because of their high visibility, they are an added factor in helping to identify envelopes of loose material from mounted pictures.

Another type of folder to be seriously considered is the suspension folder system. (Folders are suspended from tracks which are easily installed in standard file drawers *Figure 46*). This method, while a trifle more expensive to initiate, is quite economical over a long span. Because the folders glide along tracks on either side of the drawer, filing and refiling are greatly simplified and expedited: all identifying tabs remain at a constant eye-level; it is impossible for a heavy folder to slide beneath a lighter one; each folder self-adjusts to the thickness necessary to house its contents. Furthermore, the folders themselves are most sturdy.

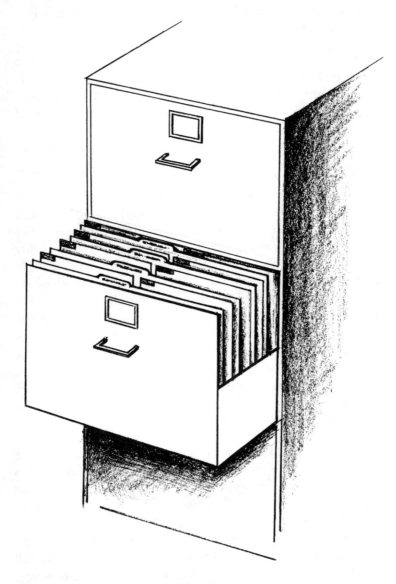

FIGURE 44

LEGAL SIZE FILE CABINET

(note placement of folders and mounted pictures)

EXPANSION FILE ENVELOPE
FIGURE 45

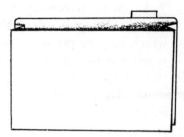

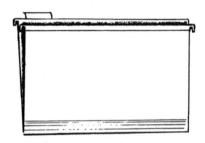

SUSPENSION FOLDER

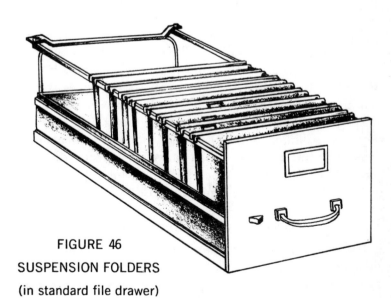

FIGURE 46
SUSPENSION FOLDERS
(in standard file drawer)

Subject Envelopes

A fourth possibility is an envelope which requires a slightly different approach to circulation procedures but which may be preferred to any of the above. The envelope is non-expanding and heavily reinforced with linen tape on three edges. There is a flap along the top (broad dimension). All loose material for one subject is placed in this envelope *except* for those pamphlets which are sturdy enough to stand alone in the subject folder. (In this case, card pockets and circulation cards are affixed to the pamphlets in addition to the standard information described on pages 71 and 74).

The subject heading is printed on the face of the envelope, right-hand side. A complete table of contents is listed on the front of the envelope, left-hand side. As contents change frequently, the listing should be printed in pencil. Also affixed to the face of the envelope, center, are a card pocket, circulation card, and date due slip (*Figure 47*). The subject envelope is now to be considered as one "pamphlet" despite the number and the assortment of its contents.

It should be noted that material treated in this manner is somewhat easier to handle in filing and refiling procedures. However, there are certain drawbacks which must be considered: (1) the preparation of subject envelopes is comparatively time-consuming and costly, (2) several subject envelopes will be needed for numerous topics since envelope capacity is limited, and (3) the tabulation of contents must be kept accurate. Use of subject envelopes greatly expedites circulation procedures (discussed in Chapter X) although here, also, a serious problem may arise.

File Folder Labels: Subject Headings

If the familiar manilla folder is used, certain points should be noted regarding labeling. A simple subject heading is typed on the label. Realizing that there will be much rear-

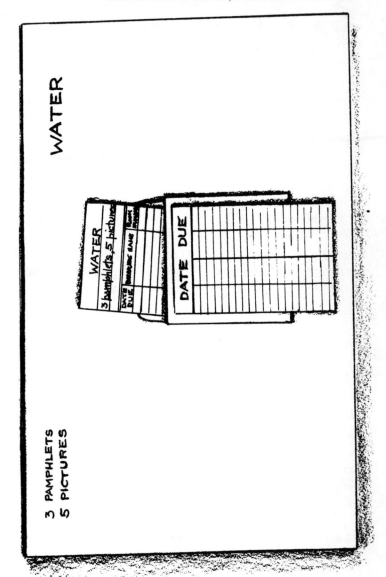

SUBJECT ENVELOPE
(Circulation Method No. 3)
FIGURE 47

ranging and revising before the librarian is satisfied with the way in which the file is functioning, there will be a strong temptation to start by hand printing the folder labels. However, this will make the job of relabeling a formidable chore when the decision is eventually made to type the proper allocations. Such a decision almost definitely will be made, no matter how far in the future it may be. Through the years, several clerks may have worked on the file labels. Therefore, the hundreds of labels will reflect this fact with many different styles of printing and writing and in many different shades of pen or pencil.

Experience has shown that the time comes when, for a neat, efficient appearance, these hand-done, erratic labels must be re-worked. Typing is the easiest method with which to achieve uniformity of the labels and consistency throughout the files. Don't write—*type at once* as new subject headings and as new folders are created.

File Folder Labels: Cross References

Another inclination to be avoided will be the suggestion to type the *"see also"* references directly on the folder label. Since the file is constantly changing, these references will also be in continual flux. Once typed, additional references cannot be added to existing labels without typing new ones. Placing labels one on top of the other adds too much thickness to the file drawers. Partial referencing creates an incomplete system which is misleading. The solution: *use folder tabs for the subject headings only.*

The *"see also"* references are typed on a colored roll-label which is then affixed to the upper left-hand corner on the front of the folder (*Figure 48*). By adopting this system, additional references can be added at any time without having to prepare a new label for each folder tab. Furthermore, there is no limitation to the space available for such notations as there is when working within the narrow tabs of the folders.

Actually, it is not essential that "*see also*" references be put on the file folders, though it does save time when actually using the files. The card catalog should contain these as well as the important "*see*" references. Users are expected to go to the card catalog first to see if there is vertical file material on a specific subject.

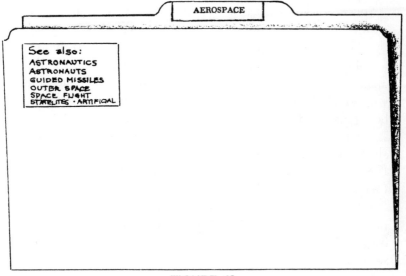

FIGURE 48

FILE FOLDER: Standard Format

File Folder Labels: Color-coding

Actual usage has proved that all folder labels should be of a different color from that of the folder itself, and from that of the mounted materials with their own self-colored labels. The file works more efficiently when colored folder labels serve as additional section separators, as well as subject identifiers. It is suggested that the color selected for labels be the same as the color-band used for vertical file materials in the card catalog (see page 84). In school libraries, particularly, consistency in the use of color-coding is of value for teaching children library routine.

File Accessories

File accessories are innumerable; it is the librarian's task to decide just what her requirements are or are likely to be. As the collection grows, and as the file grows more complex, the librarian will undoubtedly devise her own methods for simplifying filing procedures.

Some of the "extras" which may prove helpful are file jackets, file signals, out-cards, and an out-basket.

File jackets are slightly smaller than standard folders, envelope-like, but with little room for expansion. Within open-side folders, they are particularly useful for containing very small items which might fall out when the folder is being handled. They are also recommended for all folder styles to protect very small, unmounted pieces from getting "lost" or wrinkled among larger pieces within each folder. Finally, file jackets are useful for containing picture "sets" (see pages 70 and 71).

File signals are small colored metal tabs which are attached by hand to the top of the folder tab. These may be used to "signal" the fact that there are several folders on one subject.

Out-cards and out-baskets are described on page 126.

Filing the Folders

The folders are filed, as are the pictures, in simple, alphabetical order. As noted earlier, they are not meant to contain the mounted pictures, themselves. Folders are placed in *front* of all related pictures. In this way the mounted pictures are kept separate from the pamphlets (and other loose material) and then can easily be selected from the files when the subject request is just for pictures.

Since folders serve as additional guides to the proper placement of all material, it is essential that they are always in correct order within the file drawers. Misfiled folders soon cause complete havoc in the filing system. Desk assistants must be made thoroughly aware of the importance of maintaining the alphabetical order of the files. Time has shown that it is not only easier for refiling purposes to remove the folder (instead of numerous, assorted pieces) and hand it to the borrower, but also that it helps to prevent excessive handling of individual items. Personal selection, too, is made more simple for the borrower when he is able to look through the entire contents of a folder while sitting at a reading desk.

Subject envelopes are placed *within* file folders; they do not supplant the necessity of folders.

Weeding

The fact that the vertical file collection should be weeded regularly bears repeating. In addition to regular maintainance, an attempt should be made to review the *entire* file collection every two years so as to catch out-dated, damaged or misfiled material. Otherwise, the file will choke on itself and lose its prime attributes of flexibility and immediacy.

Ready availability of vertical file materials is the keystone to the effective use of this important study aid by the student body.

IX

Processing Oversized
Material

"Oversized file" denotes all those charts, maps, posters and pictures which are too large to be contained inside a regular legal size file cabinet. If such cumbersome items were to be folded to fit in the metal file, far too much bulk would be added to the individual folders. Moreover, because of their formidable appearance, they would not be used as much as they should be. Secondly, excessive folding and refolding shorten the life span of this material. Finally, once folded, they never look as fresh as they should when on display.

Housing Oversized Material

It is important to note here that no single *entirely* satisfactory system has yet been devised for housing oversized items, but there are three fairly good methods of storing such items. One is a standard blueprint file[1] which houses materials horizontally in shallow drawers. The difficulty here is in getting out the items which are toward the bottom of the drawers and are thus weighed down by those on top.

A second method for storing oversized materials is the installation of a chart rack[2] which is suspended from the ceiling. However, this device can only supplement, not replace, the above mentioned file since not all oversized pieces can be adapted for this unit. Furthermore, not all

---

[1] June Berry, "Filing Miscellaneous Materials." *School Library Journal,* February, 1962, vol. 8, p. 19.

[2] Catharine M. Williams, op. cit., pp. 41-44.

items are in enough demand to warrant being constantly at hand and constantly handled.

A third alternative to the problem of oversized materials is the construction of a cabinet such as those used in fine art and framers' shops (*Figure 49*). If space is lacking for either of the previously mentioned systems, this type of cabinet can be constructed to required specifications. Thus, otherwise unused, odd size, floor space may be utilized. Nevertheless, there are some items too large to fit even this cabinet. Normally, one fold suffices without seriously affecting display value.

In addition to housing circulating oversized material, this cabinet can also be used to store the librarian's teaching aids, large poster papers for bulletin board displays, etc.

Oversized Folders

Inside the cabinet are heavy cardboard dividers (#20 chip board, cut to fit) formed into enormous folders with expansible felt bottoms (*Figure 50*). Such folders are necessary to keep large posters from curling in on themselves and slipping under the heavy dividers, thus avoiding one serious drawback to this type of vertical file. Seven such divider-folders, each clearly marked across the top as to section covered (e.g., "A–D," "E–H," etc.), have proved sufficient for average needs.

Preparing Oversized Material

Some oversized items will be on stock sturdy enough to stand alone, others must be mounted. For these, 200#, 24″ x 36″, manilla tag, can be used since this stock gives most posters the needed additional body.

Before trimming and mounting, most oversized items will have to be smoothed of all folds and unsightly creases acquired in transit through the mail. An iron, set at the lowest temperature, is ideal.

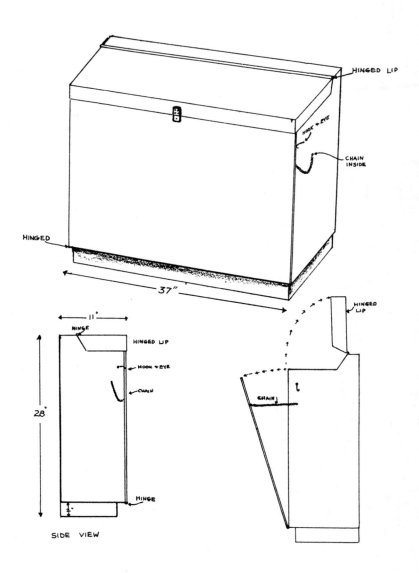

FIGURE 49

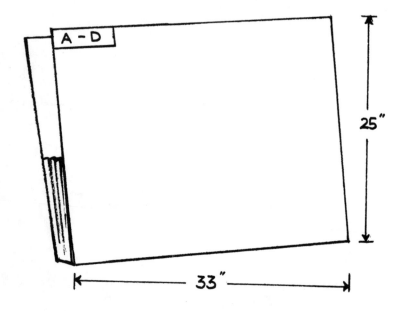

A - D

25"

33"

MATERIAL: Glued to Sides of Folder to Allow for Expansion

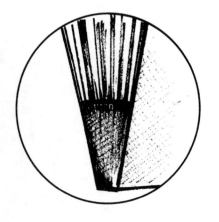

DETAIL:
Showing Expansion of Folder

FIGURE 50

A long T-square will greatly simplify and speed any trimming which might be needed on oversized sheets; attempting to work with standard rulers will be time-consuming and frustrating. (When the head, or cross-piece, of the T-square is lined up against a vertical edge, the long shank automatically provides a ruling guide for one, long, uninterrupted, horizontal line. See *Figure 51.*)

Mounting Oversized Material

Because oversized pieces are circulated in a slighty different manner than are main vertical file items (see page 124), they will not be subjected to as much handling. Therefore, the mounting of the material to backing need not be quite as solid and as strong as that of the standard pieces. Since affixing large sheets to the mounting surface is an awkward task, rubber cement and other adhesives (such as glue and paste) become ungainly to work with:

a) because of the broad surface which needs to be coated, much of the adhesive begins to dry before the job is completed;

b) too much of the adhering agent is needed to properly cover the material to be mounted and to overcome the problem noted above;

c) it is difficult to obtain the unwrinkled, flat appearance needed for attractive displays.

Accordingly, either one of two products is recommended for these mounting jobs. One, available through standard library supply sources, is a double-sided adhesive tape: a hybrid of fluid rubber cement and cellophane tape. It comes in several widths, but 1″ is recommended although ½″ to ¾″ is satisfactory. The other, obtainable from many stationery and office supply houses, is a pressure sensitive adhesive in dry *film* form. Your supplier can demonstrate its use. Both products are extremely clean to work with and easy to apply.

POSTER (before trimming)

FIGURE 51

POSTER (after trimming)

The dry mount press, of course, will solve most of the above mentioned problems.

Staples may be used in mounting oversized material, but the sides of the pieces will eventually tear from being taken in and out of the cabinet.

Problem Sized Pieces

Inevitably, no matter what type of system is selected for storing oversized material, there will be attractive pieces which are too large for the standard vertical file, too small to stand alone in the oversized cabinet, and too short to be put among the larger pieces of the blueprint file without getting lost. Ideally, an x-ray file cabinet (see page 94) will house such items. In this size, a two-drawer unit seems to be adequate for average school or small library needs. If the library lacks space to accommodate one or the other of these files, odd sized pieces can be bulked together, by subject, in common, flat, dime store bags (20" x 16½"). The bags, which are given subject headings and are labeled, must contain a complete list of contents. They can then be filed (in the standard A–Z order) in the oversized cabinet or blueprint file.

Labeling Oversized Material

Oversized file material is assigned subject headings and is labeled exactly as other vertical file material with one important exception: the designation, "oversized", should also appear on the label, otherwise many of these items will wind up being folded and filed in the standard vertical file.

Large posters such as these, housed in the oversized cabinet, furnish added visual enrichment to study units.

Mounted pictures from the vertical file can provide accurate guides for children's own dimensional projects as in this sixth grade collateral reading assignment.

X

Circulating Vertical

File Material

Length of Loan Period

One of the first decisions to be made in regard to circulating vertical file materials is whether (a) to treat them as reference materials to be used only within the library, or (b) to allow them out on loan as books are. If the latter decision is made, the librarian will then have to decide whether vertical file materials are to be required back within a specified time or whether they may be out on indefinite loan. Decisions largely depend on the type of library; the size and the value of the vertical file collection; the use which is expected of the collection; and the amount of clerical help available at the check-out desk. In school libraries, if material is retained in the classrooms, indefinite loan is entirely feasible. If certain control procedures are established, the school librarian can locate material when it is needed for other teachers. In public libraries, however, exact due dates seem to be more necessary.

Most libraries do allow circulation of vertical file materials. However, systems of circulation and of circulation control may differ widely. The reason for such differences may be due, in part, to how individual librarians view their collections, i.e., whether vertical file materials are seen as completely expendable, primarily permanent, or somewhere between the two extremes.

Charging Methods

Some librarians feel that the pamphlet collection is valuable enough to warrant separate circulation cards for each pamphlet. Some librarians even assign accession numbers. Many librarians make a sharp distinction between basically printed materials and picture items, thus maintaining two separate charging systems. Still others make no distinction whatever among the various types of vertical file items. Records are kept only of the number of pieces borrowed on a specific subject. In this last instance, many librarians feel it is necessary to keep a record of what sort of item is borrowed under the subject headings (mounted pictures, pamphlets, articles, and so forth).

Within these several different approaches, are various circulation methods which can be adapted to the individual library and its particular needs. Each librarian will have to decide how detailed the procedure is to be, but circulation need not be a complicated task. The main concern will be to prevent records from becoming burdensome.

Therefore, four methods of circulation and circulation control are listed below. The fourth, and recommended system, is described in detail.

Circulation Method No. 1

For those libraries in which each piece of the vertical file collection is charged individually, circulation is handled exactly as it is for books within each library. The only major difference is that circulation cards for each item can be made as needed. If accessioned, this number is all that is needed; if not, the title of the piece is usually written on the card.

Circulation Method No. 2

In one public library which permits vertical file materials to go out and which makes a distinction (in charging) between its picture and its pamphlet materials, the following procedure is in use:

1. A large envelope is used for circulating pictures; a smaller envelope is supplied for pamphlets.

2. All envelopes have printed forms, glued to the fronts, which provide for the following information:

No. of Pieces   **Subject**   **Card No.**   **Date Due**

3. Each envelope has been given a number.

4. A circulation card bearing this number is kept in a card pocket which has been affixed to the face of the envelope.

5. When material is being borrowed, the circulation card and the borrower's library card are placed in the book charging machine. The circulation card thus has been stamped with both the borrower's card number and the date due (*Figure 52*).

6. The desk assistant must write in, on the circulation card, the exact number of pieces and subject which are being borrowed.

7. This same information is then written in on the envelope (see above, step 2).

8. Circulation cards are filed, by number, under date due.

When material is returned to the library:

9. The number of the envelope is looked up (under date due).

10. The desk assistant checks the contents of the returned envelope against the listing on the circulation card.

11. If the count agrees, the charge is crossed off on both card and envelope (*Figure 52*).

12. If the count disagrees, and the material cannot be found by the borrower, proper adjustments must be made.

13. The card is then returned to the envelope pocket.

14. The returned materials are now ready to be refiled.

FIGURE 52

CIRCULATION CARDS

(Circulation Method No. 2)

Circulation Method No. 3

For those systems which have decided to use the filing methods described on page 98 (one envelope to contain all the loose vertical file material of each subject and individual folders for each clipping), the following circulation procedure can be employed since there is no distinction made among types of material.

In the case of *clippings*:

1. The borrower's name, subject of clipping and date due are written on a "scrap" card (any discarded catalog card).

2. The card is then interfiled with the (circulation) book cards, alphabetically by subject.

3. When the material is returned to the library, the "scrap" card can be thrown away.

4. The material is then ready for refiling.

For *subject envelopes*:

1. The card on the envelope is filled in as it would be with books.

2. The card is filed as in step 2, above.

3. When the envelope is returned to the library, its contents are checked against the information listed on the front.

4. The card is replaced in the pocket on the envelope.

5. The envelope is then ready to be returned to the vertical file.

When using *subject envelopes*, a problem may arise when the user wishes to borrow only part of the contents of an envelope. In such an instance, a complete, new envelope must be made to contain the desired pieces. The information on the face of the original envelope must be corrected accordingly before refiling.

Circulation Method No. 4

The fourth procedure is one in which the various types of materials are tabulated, both by subject and by form. Experience has shown that, as the vertical file collection grows both in scope and in value, librarians often feel the need for a somewhat more detailed circulation routine. Although this particular system is used within a school library, it can be used in any library situation. It is particularly useful in that it furnishes a tighter control of materials without taking excessive clerical time.

CIRCULATION METHOD NO. 4: CONTROL CARD

For circulation control, a separate card is used for each subject heading in the files. In addition to the subject heading which has been typed at the top of the card, there are spaces for the entry of the date on which the material is borrowed, the name of both teacher and child, and the number of each of the various types of vertical file material (*Figure 53*).

When the card is completely filled with entries, a new one is made, with circulation figures transferred, just as is done with the circulation cards of books.

The vertical file circulation control cards, filed in simple, A–Z order, are kept in their own file box or drawer. Since the box is relatively short and narrow, it can be located conveniently in, on, or near the charging desk.

This type of card seems to be the simplest and least time consuming of all:

    a. Desk assistants are not overburdened with writing numerous subject headings each time material is borrowed.

DATE	TEACHER / CHILD	PRINTED MATERIAL	MOUNTED PICTURES	UNMOUNTED PICTURES	OVERSIZE	MISC.
NORTH DAKOTA					(SUBJECT)	
VERTICAL FILE CIRCULATION:						

FIGURE 53

b. A fast fingering through the (vertical file) circulation file quickly locates those subjects which are in circulation and in which classrooms they can be found.

c. By marking the different types of items within each subject, identifying misplaced materials is made easier for both librarian and borrower. Much time is saved when it is known precisely what sort of item must be located.

d. A periodic review of the cards reveals which subjects are in demand and, conversely, which items are of little interest. The librarian thus has an accurate guide as to the direction of the vertical file collection.

CIRCULATION METHOD NO. 4:
CIRCULATING MATERIAL

The actual procedure of checking out vertical file material is rather simple.

When material is to be checked out, the method is the same whether through a teacher's written request (see *APPENDIX B*) or through direct, personal selection by the borrower.

VERTICAL FILE

Not to go home

Return all pieces together

DATE	TEACHER/CHILD	SUBJECT	PRINTED MATERIAL	MOUNTED PICTURES	UN- MOUNTED PICTURES	OVER- SIZE	MISC.

FIGURE 54

1. The appropriate (vertical file) circulation control card is selected for *each* subject being withdrawn.

2. All spaces are suitably filled in.

3. All pieces are inserted in a manilla envelope. Since protection is necessary for carrying vertical file materials outside the library, circulation envelopes should be large enough to hold the largest mounted pictures within the legal or x-ray files. The envelope should open along the broad dimension so that materials can be taken in and out with ease. Public libraries will need a rather heavy weight envelope. Some public libraries prefer to use sheets of sturdy wrapping paper to wrap materials as they are being charged. (The open edges are sealed with gummed tape.) When the material is returned to the library, the outer wrapping is discarded.

4. On the face of the circulation envelope is a mimeographed form which duplicates the information on the control card (*Figure 54*).
Note that the mimeographed form requires that *all* subject headings are to be *written* in. It would be impractical to attempt to have enough envelopes individually labeled (and filed) for every subject in the files. The flap of the envelope can contain an additional (mimeographed) note advising the borrower on display methods, etc., (*Figure 55*).

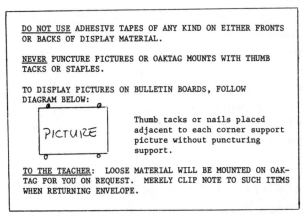

DO NOT USE ADHESIVE TAPES OF ANY KIND ON EITHER FRONTS OR BACKS OF DISPLAY MATERIAL.

NEVER PUNCTURE PICTURES OR OAKTAG MOUNTS WITH THUMB TACKS OR STAPLES.

TO DISPLAY PICTURES ON BULLETIN BOARDS, FOLLOW DIAGRAM BELOW:

PICTURE

Thumb tacks or nails placed adjacent to each corner support picture without puncturing support.

TO THE TEACHER: LOOSE MATERIAL WILL BE MOUNTED ON OAKTAG FOR YOU ON REQUEST. MERELY CLIP NOTE TO SUCH ITEMS WHEN RETURNING ENVELOPE.

FIGURE 55

5. After both circulation card and envelope are filled in, the envelope of material is given to the borrower. The card is returned to its file.

Vertical file material may not be taken out of the school except when specifically authorized by the librarian.

CIRCULATION METHOD NO. 4:
CIRCULATING OVERSIZED FILE MATERIAL

Oversized file material is usually made available at the request of the teacher since it is primarily for faculty use. When being borrowed along with other vertical file materials, such selections are entered on the appropriate circulation card and envelope; otherwise, they are marked only on the circulation card.

CIRCULATION METHOD NO. 4: RETURNED MATERIAL

File materials may be kept in the classroom as long as the teacher deems necessary. When the envelope (and oversized materials, if any) comes back to the circulation desk, the items are checked off against all entries on the envelope and the control cards; appropriate entries are crossed out with a simple pencil line. The material is then ready for refiling.

In case the teacher or the student has kept some pieces for further study, the missing items are re-charged—on both cards and envelope—with the current date. The card is returned to its place; the empty envelope is returned to the classroom. The borrower then has a record of what is still in his possession and also has the protective envelope in which to return the material when ready. *No material is accepted for return without an envelope.*

CIRCULATION METHOD NO. 4:
GRADED FILE ENVELOPES

In some instances, there will be material on one subject

that is solely in demand in one grade, and one grade, only. As mentioned elsewhere, "ideas are never limited to one grade or group." Thus, while (THE) NETHERLANDS may be studied mainly in third grade, SOUTH AMERICA in sixth, and CONSERVATION in fourth, there are always numerous requests for these subjects from other grade levels. Nevertheless, there are items presented in a way that is of interest to one grade: for instance, DAIRYING, COWS, MILK, etc., are studied in first grade. While the folders contain materials for older grades, there is no call for the several delightful pictures, story books, and pamphlets written and illustrated exclusively for the primary grade.

This "one-grade-only" material may be handled in a special manner so that it is available for the teacher when he wants it that one time a year, and yet does not overload the file folder for the remainder of the semester.

Such materials are placed in file envelopes (see page 95) which are filed *behind* all pictures in that category. On the face of the envelope is a complete inventory of the contents. When the teacher requests "his" envelope, it is removed from the file and is charged out in the accepted manner.

When he is done with it, he is able to check the material he is returning against the contents of the envelope. The entire unit is then returned to the library where it is further checked for accuracy of inventory and condition of the items within. Naturally, if new items are found to fit this unit, they will be added. If old and worn items have to be replaced, that is noted also.

If there is more than one grade teacher for the unit, the required number of special envlopes will be made for each class.

This method preserves the life of the individual pieces since they are only handled when the unit is actually being taught. Further, and a very attractive point indeed, is the fact that this sort of treatment can expedite the circulation procedure. Finally, it is double insurance that each teacher will have his unit materials ready when he calls for them.

It must be noted, however, that since this system removes the pre-selected material from general circulation, this approach must be used very sparingly.

The physical procedure for removing and for refiling materials will differ in minor details from library to library. Whether the librarian, the desk assistant, or the borrower performs the routine is largely dependent upon how the collection is housed, the location of the housing, the traffic and the staff within the library at any given moment, etc.

Two additional filing accessories which have proved to be of value are "out-guides" and an "out-basket."

Out-guides

Out-guides are legal size, brightly colored (usually orange), single oaktag sheets with a center tab strongly marked with the word, "OUT." When inserted in place of removed folders and pictures, the readily noticeable tabs serve as identifications for correct replacement of material. As items are returned to the file drawers, the out-guides are removed. The consistent use of out-guides not only speeds refiling procedures, but also helps to maintain the order of filed material (*Figure 56*).

Out-basket

Since all items are removed from the carrier envelopes upon return to the circulation desk, a container should be provided for the now loose material. A wire, legal size out-basket, placed on top of the vertical file, will conveniently hold such pieces until they can be refiled. By temporarily storing loose materials in such a basket, the likelihood of damage to individual items is greatly minimized (*Figure 56*).

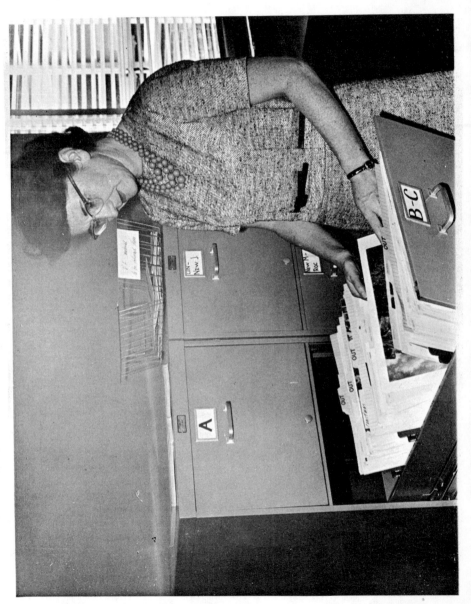

FIGURE 56: Easily seen "out-guides" in the open file drawer simplify refiling of material in the out-basket on top of the cabinet.

Appendix A
Soliciting Subject Material

In 1960, the Walter Stillman School library sent a total of 250 copies of our standard, mimeographed form letter (*Figure 19*) to the foreign embassies, legations, tourist offices, etc., listed in *Guide to Foreign Information Sources* and to the industrial development boards, tourist bureaus, chambers of commerce, etc., listed in *Sources of State Information and State Industrial Directories*. (See *APPENDIX D* for full information pertaining to the above two catalogs.)

At the time, we considered the response from both groups to be poor: approximately half of the foreign agencies and ⅔ of the domestic agencies replied, a total of 141 out of 250 mailed.

Of those responding to the request, about half seemed to have handled the letter in a purely routine way. Much of the material was unsuitable for elementary school use: i.e., heavy industrial or tourist promotional pieces, "above-grade" statistical data, and so forth. We were unable to determine whether it was the form which was at fault or if the addressed organizations simply did not have the items we were seeking.

In 1962, we tried a "saturation" mailing to all of the domestic associations once more. However, this time the form letter was specifically adapted for this purpose (*Figure 21*) and each letter was individually typewritten. The response, in both number and caliber, was gratifying. In many instances, when the agencies could not comply with our request, they wrote to inform us of this fact. Several wrote to say that they were forwarding our request to other bureaus within the state or wrote to recommend further likely sources for us to follow up.

In 1965-66, we tried the same type of mailing to foreign agencies. Another letter was written especially for these sources (*Figure 22*). In this instance, also, letters were personally typed and sent to all of the agencies listed in the above mentioned guide (excluding those with foreign addresses). The response was overwhelming both in quantity and quality.

It must be noted here that there always will be a few letters which are returned because of improper addresses: either the addressee has moved and the letter is unforwardable, or the agency no longer exists. This is true of listings found in all of the source guides with which we have worked and is a situation which cannot be avoided by the editors of such guides. However, since the number of returned pieces is negligible, it should not be a deterrent to mass mailing. We only mention this factor to alert the librarian that it is to be expected.

Again, as in the similar mailing to the domestic bureaus, a sizeable number of foreign agencies which wrote that they could not help us suggested other sources which could. The general courtesy with which our requests were received was most pleasing and satisfying.

It has been argued by some that such agencies will respond to any request, no matter how it is presented, as long as they have material and as long as it is their policy to distribute free or inexpensive materials. This is definitely not true. Our experiences have proved, beyond a doubt, that these agencies do not automatically respond to form requests. Further, our experience indicates most strongly that the *quality* of response to personally typed letters addressed to these groups —domestic and foreign—is far superior to that of processed letters.

Other important conclusions may be drawn as results of these mass mailings. We now definitely know that many of the associations listed in the two U.S. Chamber of Commerce guides do not have the type of material for which we appealed. Of the material received—from both groups—much was inappropriate for elementary school children. It must be recognized, however, that even in those instances, the vast majority did send materials which were of value as background information for the faculty, and of great worth for secondary schools and public libraries. We suggest, therefore, that if elementary school librarians decide to pursue these sources, they be prepared to receive a significant percentage of material that is not particularly useful for younger students.

Another aspect which was uncovered through the mailings, and which will serve as our own guideline for future action, is the fact that one can rely upon one's knowledge of world affairs in judging which foreign bureaus can be of service in the area of free or inexpensive materials.

1. Those countries which we know are yet underdeveloped or are in the process of organizing their governments (e.g., many newly organized African nations) generally do not have material for dissemination.

2. Those countries which are rapidly developing economically (whether industrially or as tourist centers) have material for distribution.

3. The satellite countries of Eastern Europe do not seem to have materials specifically designed for young people. In addition, the vast majority of their materials tend to present a heavily slanted viewpoint. While these pieces are interesting and have certain value within school and public libraries, they should be handled carefully, in accordance with established policy.

4. Those countries which are well developed economically seem to be able to furnish a great variety of free materials on most levels.

In collecting picture materials illustrating foreign countries, librarians will generally do well to concentrate on pictorial magazines and commercial sources for the first three categories listed above.

Satisfactory picture materials pertaining to a number of the fifty states may be obtained by writing to the bureaus listed in the source guide. However, as the vertical file collection develops, these sources become less fruitful. Although the materials which they have available do change from time to time, they appear to change slowly. Therefore, persistent mailings (certainly less than four years apart), by and large, will probably be a waste.

For non-picture materials, these agencies (both state and foreign) can—and do—supply a wealth of background information which is frequently unobtainable elsewhere.

Appendix B
Teachers' and
Children's Requests

In order to ensure the teaching staff of the availability of specific subjects at specific times, the librarian of Stillman School has devised a request form (*Figure 57*) which is filled in each month by the teacher who then returns it to the librarian. The distribution is timed so that a complete summary of teachers' needs can be passed on to the public librarian during the regular, monthly meetings of school and public librarians. Thus, because both school and public libraries have been alerted to which subjects will be in demand at any particular point of the school year, both are able to take suitable steps in having the material at hand and ready for school use.

Naturally, teachers can, and do, send for information at any time, as required. However, advance notification, in addition to aiding the libraries in their service to the schools, gives the library staff time to search for, receive, and process items not already in the files.

Further, monthly notices from the library to the teachers help to remind them that there are many ways in which the library can serve. New teachers, particularly, need to be made aware of all that a school library has to offer.

SUBJECTS PLANNED AHEAD

(Librarian expects reference not foreseen as children's interests develop.)

TEACHER_____GRADE_____DATE WANTED_____

(Please check one) Send material to me_____

I will send a child to help locate material_____

I will get material myself_____

SOCIAL STUDIES_____

_____

_____

_____

SCIENCE_____

_____

_____

ART_____

_____

LANGUAGE ARTS_____

_____

_____

FIGURE 57

Children's Requests

Although many school libraries do not permit children to browse through or to handle the material within the vertical files, Stillman School did not establish this rule until very recently. (At no time were children in the third grade and below permitted to go through the files unless they knew how to use the card catalog. A few advanced children do.) Over the years, it was found that their curiosity caused them to get too engrossed for over-long stretches of time; they frequently misfiled items; were not as careful with the pictures as they should be. Today, they must go directly to the card catalog — a sound learning experience, in any event.

When they know precisely what topics they require, they make their requests at the charging desk. The desk assistant then removes the materials from the file so that the children may peruse them at a reading table. Each pupil is free to obtain as much material at one time as he requires. The material selected by the child is charged out in the routine manner; the remainder is refiled immediately.

Browsing

Rules concerning browsing differ from library to library, but many public libraries do not permit browsing in the vertical file.

What rules to make concerning browsing depend upon the amount of clerical help available (1) to keep the files in order, (2) to repair damaged material, and (3) to replace material as necessary. Naturally, where browsing is permitted, wear and tear of materials is proportionately larger. On the other hand, there is no question but that borrowers often are better served when they can search for materials themselves. They frequently locate materials in which they are interested and which they would not have found otherwise. (Just as library patrons like to browse in the open shelves for books, so do they like to browse in the vertical file.) If at all feasible, browsing by the patrons, child and adult alike, is recommended. However, the librarian must be prepared to have extra time spent in maintaining the files.

Appendix C
Table of Equipment
and Supplies

(not including standard library equipment)

For Correspondence
    Letterheads, 8½" x 11"
    Post Cards, U.S.
    Window envelopes, #10
                Optional:
    Rubber stamps: "Please address reply
               to my attention!"
               Library name and ad-
               dress (for envelopes)

For Inventory/Reference File
    'Scrap" catalog cards (or 3" x 5" cards)
    Card box

For Processing Vertical File Material
    Mounting board: 14-pt., manilla tag;
                   cut 10" x 14½"
                   200# manilla tag;
                   cut 24" x 36"
    Rubber cement
    Thinner
    Adhesive "pick-up"
    Perforated adhesive cloth, 1"
    Double-sided adhesive tape, 1"
    Staples
    Editors' shears
    Single-edge razor blade and sheath holder
    Paper cutters (2)
    Steel-edge ruler
    Pencils, #2
    Plastic triangle, 12"
    T-square, 36"
    Red (and assorted colors) nylon-tip pens
    Roll-labels, manilla
    Sturdy, broad, chemical resistant, work surface
                Optional:
    Dry mount press
    Backing cloth
    Fixative spray
    Transparent plastic laminating sheets

For Displaying Pictures
    Wire nails, ¼"

For Cataloging
    Catalog cards, color-banded
    Rubber stamps: "Vertical File"
                   "Oversized File"
                   "X-ray file" (if necessary)

For Housing and Filing
    Legal size file cabinet
    Oversized file cabinet
    Legal size file folders
    Legal size file jackets
    Legal size "out-cards"
    Legal size "out-basket"
    Roll labels, blue
    Plain paper bags, 20" x16½"
                         Optional:

    File signals
    X-ray file cabinet

For Circulation
    Circulation control cards
    Card box
    Circulation envelopes, 12" x 18"
    Circulation envelope forms (mimeographed)
                         Optional:
    "Teacher's Request" forms (mimeographed)

Appendix D
Guides to Sources of Free and Inexpensive Materials

All guides give full bibliographic data to use in ordering.
Users may notice some duplication of listings when working with two or more guides since the same suppliers are common to all. However, each guide has its own merits which are independent of any duplications which may occur.

BRUCE MILLER PUBLICATIONS, Box 369, Riverside, California, 92502.

> *Let's Celebrate a Holiday,* 1966.
>
> *Sources of Free and Inexpensive Pictures for the Classroom,* 1965.
>
> *Sources of Free and Inexpensive Teaching Aids,* 1965.
>
> *Sources of Free Pictures,* 1967.
>
> *Sources of Free Travel Posters and Geographic Aids,* 1965.

Above publications at 50¢ each can be of use in first starting a picture/pamphlet file. Listings are few and there is some duplication among the publications. Number of sources not given. No indexes. Items are arranged by subject; a few are graded. *Let's Celebrate a Holiday* and *Sources of Free Pictures* are largely indexes by subject to material in periodicals (1961-1965 and 1963-1966 respectively).

CHAMBER OF COMMERCE OF THE UNITED STATES, Foreign Commerce, Foreign Policy Department, 1615 H Street, N.W., Washington, D.C., 20006.

> *Guide to Foreign Information Sources,* 1964, 25¢. Chiefly names and addresses of offices maintained by foreign countries within the United States where one can write for free material.

CHAMBER OF COMMERCE OF THE UNITED STATES, State Chamber of Commerce Service Department, 1615 H Street, N.W., Washington, D.C., 20006.

> *Sources of State Information and State Industrial Directories,* 1964, 25¢. Names and addresses where state materials can be obtained, mostly free of charge.

DOVER PUBLICATIONS, 180 Varick Street, New York, New York 10014.

> *Free and Inexpensive Educational Aids,* 3rd edition, 1966, edited by Thomas J. Pepe, $1.75. Highly selective, annotated and graded list arranged under nineteen broad subject headings. Excellent index. More than 1,700 items listed, from 476 sources, evaluated by a

number of teachers actually using the materials. "88% free, 9% less than 25¢."

EDUCATORS PROGRESS SERVICE, Randolph, Wisconsin, 53956.

Elementary Teachers Guide to Free Curriculum Materials, 24th edition, 1967, edited by Patricia H. Suttles, $8.75. An important guide for the elementary school librarian, since most items cited can be used with grades 1 through 9. There are a number above this level, and a number for teacher use only. Mostly pamphlets, with a few maps, posters and realia included. 1,497 selected items from 565 sources are given under broad subject headings close to library terminology. 756 new items. Separate title and subject indexes. Good annotations. Revised annually. All new titles are starred, thus making it easy to check when ordering from year to year.

Educators Guide to Free Science Materials, 8th edition, 1967, edited by Mary H. Saterstrom and John W. Renner, $8.25. Largely films and filmstrips but does include some pamphlets, charts and posters which are useful in the vertical file. 1,666 selected items, 528 of which are new in this edition.

Educators Guide to Free Social Studies Materials, 7th edition, 1967, compiled and edited by Patricia H. Suttles, $8.50. Organized by media with color coding of pages, making it easy to locate specific kinds of materials. A total of 2,357 selected items, 707 new in this edition, 565 sources listed. 437 items (yellow pages) for the vertical file.

Educators Index of Free Materials, 1967, $24.00. This is a card file, with sources and items listed under broad subjects. An easy-to-use source index.

ESTHER DEVER, P.O. Box 186, Grafton, West Virginia, 26354.

Sources of Free and Inexpensive Educational Materials, 3rd edition, 1965, by Esther Dever, mimeographed, $5.25. Annotated listing, arranged alphabetically under 77 subject areas. Home Economics and Social Studies are subdivided. Includes audio-visual materials as well as pamphlets for all grade levels. Some grading. No index. Over 1,500 sources, with more than 3,700 free items. Needs careful evaluation of materials as this is not a very selective listing. Lack of index complicates usage.

FAXON COMPANY, F. W. Faxon Company, 83-91 Francis Street, Back Bay, Boston, Massachusetts, 02115.

Index to Illustrations, 1967, by Jessie Croft Ellis, $12.50. A subject index to illustrations contained in twenty-one books and seven periodicals. The cut-off date for the latter is generally 1960. A fairly wide range of subjects is presented. A number of subjects are on Americana. Religious librarians will find the listings under "Asia Minor" and "Archaeology" of particular interest. Although this is not a guide to inexpensive materials, librarians should know that an index such as this is available.

FEARON PUBLISHERS, 2165 Park Boulevard, Palo Alto, California, 94306.

Selected Free Materials for Classroom Teachers, 2nd edition, 1967, edited by Ruth H. Aubrey, $1.75. Carefully selected, annotated and graded items grouped under "nationally recognized curriculum topics." A number of educators worked on the selections. Over 570 sources of free materials (mostly pamphlets) are listed. Very easy to use with source given in the same paragraph as names and descriptions of items. Compact, well indexed.

GEORGE PEABODY COLLEGE FOR TEACHERS, Division of Survey and Field Services, Nashville, Tennessee, 37203.

Free and Inexpensive Learning Materials, 13th biennial edition, 1966, edited by Jack W. Miller, $2.00. Carefully selected with brief annotations of more than 4,000 items. 128 subjects listed alphabetically with many "see also" references. The subjects chosen are "generally parallel to the units taught in elementary and secondary schools." Includes a number of government pamphlets. Many sources are listed for further bibliographies on specific subjects. A few items are graded, but not many are marked for the elementary school. No index.

NATIONAL EDUCATION ASSOCIATION, Department of Audiovisual Instruction, 1201 Sixteenth Street, N.W., Washington, D.C., 20036.

Learning from Pictures, by Catharine M. Williams, 1963, $4.50. Exceedingly helpful book for the teacher with guidelines for choosing pictures to use in the classroom. Contains both a "Primary Source List to Producers of Pictorial Materials" with brief notations of items available from 138 sources and subject index to materials supplied by sources cited. 3rd edition is scheduled to be published in 1968, $4.50.

PAN AMERICAN UNION, Sales and Promotion Division, Washington, D.C., 20006.

Publications Catalog: 1967-1968. Free. Arranged alphabetically by subject. Indexed. Publications in English, Spanish, Portuguese and French are listed. "American Republics," "Commodity," and "Young American" series are inexpensive and useful in schools.

SCARECROW PRESS, INC., 52 Liberty Street, P.O. Box 656, Metuchen, New Jersey, 08840.

Illustrations Index, 2nd edition, 1966, by Lucille E. Vance and E. M. Tracey, $12.00. A subject index to illustrations contained in nine books and fifteen periodicals. The latter "represent many fields of interest." Magazines indexed are mostly from 1950 through June, 1963. Good coverage of costume. Most are photographs, but some paintings, charts and drawings are included. A tool for locating hard-to-find pictures.

SPECIAL LIBRARIES ASSOCIATION, Picture Division, 31 East Tenth Street, New York, New York, 10014.

Picture Sources, 2nd edition, 1964, edited by Celestine G. Frankenberg, $6.75. The preface of the book states that it "is not intended as a source for teachers," but librarians should be aware of its existence in case some special school project requires more than the usual materials. Sources grouped by nine broad categories, plus one chapter on "General Picture Collections" and one on "Specialized Collections." Contains 703 entries. Each entry gives name of library, museum, organization or company with brief statements concerning collection. Some pictures are available on a loan basis; many can be reproduced for a fee. There are excellent bibliographies of "Picture-Finding Tools" for each subject area.

STATE COLLEGE OF IOWA, Extension Service, Cedar Falls, Iowa, 50613.

Free Learning Materials for Classroom Use; An Annotated List of Sources with Suggestions for Obtaining, Evaluating, Classifying and Using, 1967, by Guy Wagner and Dorian Mark, $1.50. Presents good discussions of the value of the vertical file and of selection criteria for free material. An annotated and graded listing of about 1,275 selected items from more than 400 sources. Includes a subject index to sources.

WILSON COMPANY, H. W. WILSON COMPANY, 950 University Avenue, New York, New York, 10452.

Vertical File Index: A Subject and Title Index to Selected Pamphlet Material, $8.00 yearly subscription, monthly except August. One of the most up-to-date basic sources. According to the foreword, this publication is "considered to be of interest to general libraries." It lists about 3,200 pamphlets yearly; many items annotated. There are few free pamphlets. Few are of value for the elementary school vertical file. A good guide to pamphlets of value for faculty use on all levels.

WORLD AFFAIRS MATERIALS, Brooklyn College, Brooklyn, New York, 11210.

Free and Inexpensive Materials on World Affairs, 1965, by Leonard S. Kenworthy, $1.50. Grouped by broad subject headings, some geographical. Good coverage of United Nations. A few brief annotations. "All items listed may be obtained for 75¢ or less. Many of the items are free." No index. Most items listed were published after 1960. New edition planned for 1968 with Richard Birdie as collaborator.

SELECTION AIDS FOR GOVERNMENT PAMPHLETS

Even though most government pamphlets are above level for the elementary school, there are a number which can supply reliable supplementary material and should not be overlooked. A very important source for the high school and adult library patron.

COLUMBIA UNIVERSITY PRESS, 136 South Broadway, Irvington-on-Hudson, New York, 10533.

A Popular Guide to Government Publications, 3rd edition, 1968, by W. Philip Leidy, $12.00. A carefully selected and annotated list of about 3,000 pamphlets and books, listed under 105 subject entries with many *"see also"* references. Contains some popular titles published by the Pan American Union. Evaluations often include some comparisons with other titles in the specific field. Delightfully written.

U. S. SUPERINTENDENT OF DOCUMENTS, Government Printing Office, Washington, D.C., 20402.

Monthly Catalog, $4.50 a year. "Most complete listing of currently issued Government publications" arranged alphabetically by issuing department, bureau and agency. Includes Congressional publications. Indexed monthly with annual index in December issue. Section called "Previews" gives important forthcoming titles.

Monthly Checklist of State Publications, issued by U. S. Library of Congress, Processing Department, $3.00 a year. Arranged alphabetically by states, territories and insular possessions of the United States. Includes annual index of subjects and titles.

Subject Price Lists, sent free upon request, covers 46 subjects such as National Parks, Indians, Weather. Many of the new publications listed are well annotated. "Revised approximately once a year."

Selected List of Government Publications, free, issued semimonthly. Names put on the mailing list upon request. Contains "newly issued as well as still popular publications."

PAMPHLET JOBBERS

Use of a jobber simplifies ordering and payment procedures but often results in extensive delays.

BACON PAMPHLET SERVICE, East Chatham, New York, 12060.

Free brochures listing titles with brief annotations. Orders accepted for any pamphlets except free ones, handling charge for orders of less than $5.00.

VERTICAL FILE MATERIALS, Box 481, Lincoln, Nebraska, 68501.

Publishes well annotated list of pamphlets eight times a year, annual subscription, $1.70. Orders accepted for any pamphlets, including free ones. Service charge "4¢ for first copy of any title, 2¢ for each additional copy of the same title"; no service charge on government pamphlets and some others.

THE WILLIAM-FREDERICK PRESS; Pamphlet Distributing Company, Inc., 55 East 86 Street, New York, New York, 10028.

Orders accepted for any pamphlets, including free ones. Service charge of "15 cents per title (not per copy)," plus postage charges.

OTHER SOURCES TOO NUMEROUS TO LIST INDIVIDUALLY

Librarians may notice that guides to free sources occasionally are published for the general public. These inexpensive books can be of value to consumers seeking information on specific products, vacation areas, etc. However, such guides are of limited use for vertical file collections.

MAGAZINES (many list free and inexpensive materials)

MUSEUM PUBLICATIONS

SPECIAL SUBJECT BIBLIOGRAPHIES

INDEX